Stopford Augustus Brooke

The Unity of God And Man

And other Sermons

Stopford Augustus Brooke

The Unity of God And Man
And other Sermons

ISBN/EAN: 9783744744331

Printed in Europe, USA, Canada, Australia, Japan

Cover: Foto ©Thomas Meinert / pixelio.de

More available books at **www.hansebooks.com**

THE UNITY OF GOD AND MAN

And Other Sermons

PREACHED AT BEDFORD CHAPEL, BLOOMSBURY,

BY THE

REV. STOPFORD A. BROOKE, M.A.

BOSTON:
GEORGE H. ELLIS, 141, FRANKLIN STREET,
MDCCCLXXXVI.

PREFACE.

THE Sermons included in this volume have appeared at various times, in a private publication, and I have thought that the public might, perhaps, care to read them. They have been carefully revised and corrected.

The two discourses on Joshua do not include any statement concerning the authenticity of the history, but the remarks at the beginning of the following sermon on Lot and Abraham state the way in which I look upon, and consider these early Old Testament stories.

STOPFORD A. BROOKE.

1, MANCHESTER SQUARE,
  May 1, 1886.

CONTENTS.

	PAGE
The Unity of God and Man	6
Do. *(continued)*	14
Do. *(continued)*	23
The Wandering Sheep	34
Eternal Punishment	45
The Communion of Saints	61
Atonement	71
Do. *(continued)*	82
Do. *(continued)*	94
The Life and Character of Joshua	110
Do. *(continued)*	126
The Later Choice of Life	143
False Fervour of Heart	155
The Fervour that seeks Monotony	166
The Education of Fervour of Spirit	177
Youth.—Fervent in Spirit	188
Middle Age.—Not Slothful in Business	201
Old Age.—Serving The Lord	212

SERMONS.

[June 7, 1885.]

THE UNITY OF GOD AND MAN.

"I and my Father are one."—JOHN x. 30.

This mighty saying proclaims by the lips of Jesus the ancient truth suggested in the first of the Hebrew books, that man is the image of God. It is the highest of the disclosures made by Jesus concerning Man. Indeed, all that he has told us of humanity is contained in it. Embodied now and then in casual phrase by prophets of other races, hidden in myth and legend, Jesus was the first who declared it roundly, clearly, boldly, and left it to mankind. And it was not understood by those who came after him. They could not believe that he said it as a man, in the name of humanity. Therefore, not wishing to deny his words, they declared that Jesus said it, as God, about himself and God.

The true, and the more practical view is, that Jesus, when he said these words, and others of the same meaning, said them, knowing and feeling himself to be nothing more than a man; said in them that which was, in idea, true of all the human race, which ought to be true of every man, and which in the future will be true of all men. There is none who, having grown to the measure of the stature of the fulness of Christ, will not be able hereafter to say with him—I and my Father are one.

It is the right and destiny of the human race which are proclaimed in these words—Man is at one with God. That is the Magna Charta of our religion; the idea by which we live, towards which we strive; the idea which will certainly become fact for all of us. It was the voice of Jesus; the voice of his revelation. It is the voice now in our hearts whereby we cry—Abba, Father; and our conviction of it is supported by the daily growth of the spiritual life.

I will take it here as the theory by which we may best explain the conceptions man in general has conceived of God. There are other theories, of course, both Christian and unchristian, spiritual and materialistic; but as this was the assumption, the revelation, of Jesus, let us see what it does when we bring up to it for explanation the main ideas of God which mankind possesses.

We certainly have conceptions of God. How did we gain them? According to this theory—according, in another way of stating it, to this revelation of Jesus—we gain them from God Himself in us. The divine attributes belong to us in part. We realize them imperfectly, portions of them; we are conscious of their imperfection in us; conscious of their partial quality in us; and immediately we desire and imagine their perfection, and in this effort we dimly conceive Deity. The idea of God in us is the idea of our own spiritual nature, made pure and infinite in thought. It is not in a figure that we are like God, but in reality. We conceive His attributes because we share in them.

Again, God is intelligence, pure intelligence. How do we come to think that? We conceive it by and through our own intelligence. Through our limited intelligence we can conceive the illimitable Intelligence—because what there is of it in us is the same in kind as it is in God. The light and fire and life of thought of which we are aware, through their partial manifestation in ourselves, we proceed to conceive of as absolute and perfect, and in doing so we think of God and shape Him before us—we shape supreme Intelligence.

Again, how do we know of God's goodness, of His love? Not from without us, not primarily from revelation, but by the goodness and love we have within us! *They* are God's character in us; and when we are lifted over sin in conquest, or are ardent in the hour of some great sacrifice, then we know that we are so far—in the action of the powers of goodness and love—at one with God; and with a rush of unconscious faith, we multiply our love and goodness infinitely, and behold our God.

And when that inward law within, whereby we approve of righteousness and hate sin, speaks clear and loud, and calls us to obey it; when abiding in it we are conscious of an infinite Right and Truth, of a mighty authority without us, and in us, whereby all things are bound, to which God Himself binds Himself, and which His will, self-determined, obeys—why have we these thoughts? What means this vast and sublime imperative? How is it that we know it?

It is because we are partakers of God's moral nature, because we are made in His image, because we and the Father are one.

It is not we alone then who have wrought this, who have

made this God out of our own fancies, built Him up out of our wants and thoughts, developed Him, while He has no real existence! There are folk whose intellect that theory satisfies; there are others who are afraid that theory is true. I am sorry for both of them; but death at least will settle the questioning of the one and the trouble of the other; and death is not far away. But for us, it is better to have another faith while we live, and to hear in our hearts those words—" O fools and slow of heart to believe all that the prophets have spoken." Our theory, our faith is—That it is God who, thinking through our thought, loving through our love, has built up in man man's thought of Him, woven into our nature our love of Himself, our knowledge of Him as love. It is the Father in the child who has made known the Father. We and the Father are one.

Others say that it is from without us, from the universe and its work on the perceptions, that we conceive God.

In truth God is in the universe; in everything His thought appears to us! But appears to what? If the universe be only matter, of course it speaks only to matter in us; and there it ends for the materialists. They are now a few and feeble folk, and need not be considered. But if it be Thought that energizes in the universe, why then, it speaks to thought and its powers in us; and we understand what is doing in the universe because we are capable of doing the same kind of things ourselves. It is because we can ourselves create, that we can comprehend creation. It is because we can design, apportion means to an end, conceive a whole, that we can discover design, see the means whereby Nature, as we call it, reaches its ends, find out and grasp the ideas on which the whole is built, and then approach the conception of the whole. It is because we are wise within to feel beauty, and to reverence what is noble, that we see beauty in the universe, and bend before its sublimity in the loving awe which is the true mother of all the arts. Here also we see God by God's own light in us, because we are by nature at one with Him. The glory of God's thought in the universe is seen by the light of thought in ourselves. It is not from the outward we gain our conception of God in Nature, it is from God Himself in us.

But God is infinite, and men say, He is incomprehensible by the finite. As a whole, and at present, yes! But apart from the truth that we are not, in one sense of the word, finite at all, for we are destined to endless development and life—our existence being conterminous with the existence of God—there is this also to be said, that our thought and love and noble power (being, as we assume, of God,) have always the quality of their source. Their essence is always the same, however vast the distance between the degrees of them. The infinite is always the infinite.

We cannot call God love without feeling love, nor imagine Him as thought without having thought; and love is the same in kind for ever and in all things; and so is thought. The smallest conception is, by its very nature, always infinite. The faintest movement of love is eternal. The heat of the candle is the same in kind as the heat of the sun, and *is* the light and the heat of the sun.

Moreover, we do conceive infinity; and we could not conceive it had we not a nature which had kinship with it. We ascribe it to God, because we are of its character. We believe in it, because we possess its powers in the midst of our limitations. We aspire towards more and more of it, because we are capable of more and more of it.

In all high action for unattained truth; in original conceptions; in their creation into form; in imagination's rush beyond the stars; in the long desire after ideal beauty; in the unwearied pursuit of knowledge; in the dreams of unknown joy; in the unfathomable depths of human love; in the martyr's moral power when he dies for truth; in that might of the soul which conquers and despises all the force of the world; in the immeasurable rapture of men in death when they see God and feel the first leap within them of the immortal life; in the mystery of awe we have amid the storm; in the absoluteness of our quiet when we are satisfied with the peace of the summer; in the infinite delight which eternal beauty, seen through all art, bestows on us and in the inspiration which it kindles; in our certainty of an infinite of beauty beyond all that Nature presents to us and art embodies, and in our immediate creation of the conception of that beauty; in the power of faith that can remove mountains; in a thousand thousand things—each a fact of our actual life—the spirit is always rushing beyond its limits, knows that it has wants, and an end which only more and more of the infinite, more of that which it has in part, can set at rest. Well, what theory best explains these perceptions, these conceptions? They are facts. It is known that the human race has felt and thought these things. Is it the theory which says they are developed in the movement of eternal matter, or is it our theory—that God Himself, being infinite, has entered into His children, developed in them the thought of His own infinity, and that they themselves are infinite in Him?

That at least is our view. The infinite of God has itself in us. It knows itself in us; we are one of its forms. It is not a belief of it that we have, it is an actual feeling, and it becomes a fact of consciousness. It is a mistake to call ourselves finite. We are God's children, of His nature, born in His image, at one with the Father, and infinite in Him.

This, then, is the most glorious truth which we can believe and know. If God be the absolute goodness, if He be the source and end of truth and love and justice, then there is no good so great as to be like Him; no grace so great as to be loved by Him; no gift so supreme as the gift of Himself. To have intellectual and moral kinship with Him, to have a heart beating with a love that resembles His, to be a spirit that hungers and thirsts to be at one with His righteousness, to grow into union with His perfection, to be His children through unity of Nature—all other joys and blessings are, like rivers that stream into the ocean, borne into and accomplished in that sea of happiness. "In His presence is fulness of joy, and at His right hand are pleasures for evermore." Therefore, our chief work in life is to grow out of our imperfect likeness to God into His perfect likeness; to know absolutely Him, and His life—in Himself, and in the universe, and in ourselves—in thought and love, in form and action. And this, our chief work, will become our chief delight.

For only as we are like Him can we enjoy Him and His universe. Only as we realize more of that divine life to which we aspire can we get the pleasure out of it. It is the pure in heart who see purity, and whom it makes happy. It is those who love who can know love, and to whom it is unbounded joy. It is they who are of the truth, who hear truth's voice, to whom it is the music of the world. It is they who see, and know, and hear these things who become consciously at one with God. God is ours when we become God, if I may be allowed to use a paradox. As we grow up into Him, the union becomes personal. He is here, in our hearts. We feel His touch upon the chords of the spirit. He mingles with us, thinks through our thought, speaks in our speech, sees through our eyes, loves in our love; and is beyond them all—as holy fire, swift inspiration, educating watchfulness, tender care. Our pleasures are for evermore! Being like Him, we rejoice in Him.

Then, having learnt to rejoice in His moral and spiritual being, we pass on to rejoice in His ideas, and in the beauty into which they are shaped. We understand and love the universe. Understand it! As the Natural philosopher? No! We may not know all its secrets, nor be able to analyze it. But glorious as is the pleasure of the philosopher if he keep his reverence and be not the slave of mere knowledge, we, even without scientific knowledge, can see the thoughts on which the universe is built as the poet sees them, as Job saw them of old, as millions saw them long before one ray of science illumined the world. These majestic thoughts fill us with awe, and exalt us with their glory. God's thought has become one with us, and then, rejoicing in His thought, we pass onwards into union with the passion and love which, flowing from God's joy, pervade the universe. We feel, and know why we feel, the beauty of the world. It is God's own loveliness and harmony which from all Nature streams through us, and disturbs us into joy, and excites us with illimitable variety, illimitably inter-woven. The lowliest flower speaks to us of Him, the mightiest mountain lifts its head in prayer to Him, the sea chants of His beauty, and the everlasting stars reply. And all that we feel, we feel because we are His children, because we and the Father are one.

Lastly, from the universe, we turn to all mankind. It, too, is pervaded with God; and when we love and rejoice in Him, we begin to love and rejoice with Him in humanity. This was the thought that made the very life of Jesus. He saw—in all the pure original feelings of man, in all the ways that love acted between men and men, in the desires and longings of the soul, in the imagination, conscience, intellect of man—his Father's nature and qualities, believed in them in us, loved them, and rejoiced. Men and his Father were one, as he and his Father were one.

Therefore Jesus had an undying hope, the hope that we should possess, and by which we should live. It was more than hope, it was certainty. He knew, and rejoiced to know, that, when the evil in man was overthrown, every conscious spirit that had ever been born into the earth, would come at last to say with his own conviction—"I and the Father are one."

[June 14, 1885.]

THE UNITY OF GOD AND MAN.

"I and my Father are one."—JOHN x. 30.

It was perhaps the worst evil of the old monarchies and imperialisms that kings and emperors were practically thought to have a nature different from that of their subjects, and to be severed from them by a great gulf; and it was none the better but rather the worse for humanity when that notion was transferred to a whole class, as to the noblesse of France; and the king was considered to be the first gentleman in the caste. For then, not only one, but a great number of men and women were degraded by this false opinion, that is, by an opinion which was against Nature; lived by it in a ruinous isolation, and did the deeds which naturally flowed from it—and their deeds were abominable. It was no wonder, considering that in France this view was more plainly attacked and its iniquities more painfully felt than in other parts of Europe, that the Revolution broke out first in France. And the first thing it said was said by St. Paul at Athens, and was derived from Jesus Christ. "God hath made of one blood all nations on the face of the whole earth."

It was natural, since men calling themselves Christians came to take up that imperialistic view, that it should be said to belong to the origins of Christianity. But that was not the case. It stole into Christianity from the East, and was developed then by the Imperialism of Rome; and in accordance with it God was made an Emperor. He was divided in nature from His subjects; He might do as He willed with them, because He had the power; and they could only approach Him through the ministers of His court. This is a view which still continues, and it is as false and as fatal to a true religion or a true society as the view taken by the king and the nobles was to the society and the policy which the Revolution overthrew. No truce should be kept with that view; the sword of the intellect and the spirit should never be sheathed till it is overthrown; and if in order to destroy it we have to go through a period of partial denial of God and abjuration of religion, we can bear that trouble, if only this evil doctrine be overthrown. It seems we must go through such a period, for indeed we are living in it; but at least, some of us may keep our heads and guard our hearts, and—without dropping into the curious condition of Atheism, or into that ill-fortuned decay of love and of imagination which comes from a denial of all religion—realize the higher view of God and human society to which even Science itself, the very cause of so much of our disbelief, is leading us day by day. When the idea of God as conceived by Christ is clear, and the idea of Man that is contained in it is fully grasped, no one will dream of disbelieving in God, or of thinking that any man is capable of altogether dying.

It is, I believe, considered a mark of high and emancipated intellect, and, strangely enough, of bold imagination, even of noble emotion, to have given up the faiths of God and of immortality. It is, in reality, want of intellectual grasp, or enfeebled imagination, or the dwindling of the powers of the heart which have chiefly produced the denial of God and of immortality on the side of unbelief, and the base views of God and of immortality on the side of orthodox theology. I do not know which is most sorrowful—to say that there is no God, or to say that He is like an irresponsible Eastern Emperor; to say that there is no immortality, or to say that we are, for the most part, to be immortal with the devil in eternal division from God. The denial is perhaps the saddest of the two, for it finally leaves us face to face with pessimism.

But both vanish before the view of God in His kinship to man—the view of Jesus Christ—that which is laid down in the great saying, spoken by a man in behalf of humanity, "I and the Father are one." Man is then by nature the child of God, and not the child of the devil. There is an individual unity of nature between God and man. Man cannot be separated from God, nor God from man. The child of any father on earth may go astray, wander far from his home, himself deny his origin, do all that his father dislikes and hates—but the tie is not finally broken. The father, unless he be false to fatherhood, recognizes his relationship all through the forgetfulness of the son, and says to himself, as he thinks in sorrow and solitude—"Yet he is my son, mine own. When he returns he shall find himself at home; nay more, I cannot bear his absence; I will seek him till I find him, and make him at one with me in love and in character. He must suffer, but his suffering shall burn up his evil. But I will never deny him, never fling him away. I should be false to myself if I could do or even think that wrong."

Is God different from that; less noble, less worthy, less loving than the fatherhood of earth? No; infinitely more noble, worthy and loving! There is no earthly tie so close as that which binds God to His children on earth. It were more easy to annihilate the universe than to destroy that immortal bond. The Child and the Father are one.

And to be a father, what is it? It is to give our own nature and our own life to beings kindred with ourselves, and to educate them into a full likeness to ourselves. The bond is not only a bond of birth, it is a spiritual, intellectual, moral and loving bond. And God is Father when, having created us akin to Himself, he educates us into union with His intelligence, His righteousness, His love, and into those powers in Him by which He creates all that gives joy and embodies beauty; so that we may be His fellow workmen in the universe, immortal as Himself, and only less infinite in that while He always is, we are always becoming.

If these things be true, what is our religion? It is to believe in this bond between us and God, to live in the love of it, to feel all the emotions that flow from it, and to do all the deeds to which this faith and love impel us. It is to worship Him whom we thus conceive; to worship a God akin to us, whose moral, intellectual, loving nature is the same in kind as our own; who is the perfection of our spiritual being; who is within us a Presence so vital, powerful and creative, that we are enabled to grow into His very image; and who, in proportion as we grow, communicates to us, in fuller and fuller life, His own goodness, power, love and joy; and with them, and of them, His truth and harmony.

So, then, the true worship of God is to become that which we worship; to draw nearer to Him as the sun whence light and purity and wisdom and power stream into our souls. It is not to tremble before Him, but to have the joy and boldness and humility of love, and to do His will because we are certain it is for the perfection of the race of man. It is to bear all that comes upon us of suffering or of trial, knowing that what is borne is for the use and good of the whole of humanity. It is always to believe in His order and His love, and to abide patiently the end. It is to feel His quickening life within us, making us immortal; and to do the works meet for immortality. It is to be impassioned for more and more of Him within us. It is by purity to see Him, by love to dwell in Him, by truth to know Him, in reverence to understand Him, in humility to rejoice in Him, in joy to abide in His work, in power to do His work; and in all, to know and be ravished by His everlasting beauty.

Is that a personal religion which terrifies or depresses, which tends to superstition, which nurtures ignorance, lessens love, enfeebles intelligence, degrades our powers, fetters reason, or injures conscience?

On the contrary, it uplifts us into courage, for we fear nothing but doing wrong. It raises us into joy, for it gives us endless life, and that life is love. It destroys superstition, which is the offspring of ignorance and fear of God, for it makes us know God and love what we know, and perfect love casts out all fear. It kindles love, for it reveals eternal beauty.

It makes us reverence all intelligence, for every spark of intellect is divine—His own, who is the Fount of Thought, the beginning and the end of Truth. It sets the reason free, for to use it is to use His gift. It delivers the conscience when it is injured by theological authority, for what God gave we may not deny. It ennobles the powers of man, for we use them as the powers of God.

And so indeed He wills it should be with us, who begat us of His own good will, and cherished us in youth, and trained us to be men, and keeps us through old age to His Eternal Kingdom—God, with whom we are at one for ever. This is our personal religion! What our religion, on the same grounds, ought to be in our life with men, I shall speak of next Sunday. Meanwhile, let me dwell for a little on what power this union with God should give us in the course of human life.

All our true life is made up of work, and joy, and sorrow, and growth. With regard to Work, into which we shape all our inward being, it is, in this idea, the work also of God. It is He who works through our hand in manual labour; it is He who speaks through all we do in business; it is He who shapes our thought and passion on the canvass, into the marble, through the music that we make, and the buildings that we frame for the worship or the use of men. It is He who writes with us on all the subjects of human thought and experiment, who leads us into all science, who forms the drama and builds the poem. It is He who with us heals the sick, and preaches the Gospel, and frames the law, and defends the right, and governs the nation—and in that belief all work is sanctified, guarded by conscience, freed from the world, ennobled by an ideal, enkindled by love, triumphant in failure, finished with joy even though it be finished on the Cross.

And as to Joy, it does not, if we hold it within this idea of natural union with God, remain within ourselves, nor end in selfishness. It passes beyond the earth to become gratitude in Heaven. We lose the chances of its becoming evil, when we bind it up with God. We will have none of it for which we cannot praise God with a quiet mind. And, day by day, as we praise Him for pure joy, we find more for which to praise Him; we fill the world with God, and walk with Him. His is the freshness of the morning, and the rest of eventide. His the beauty of the woodlands and the waters, of the mountains and the clouds that love them, of the deep sea, and the multitudes of the flowers, and His the language of the kindly earth and the ancient Heavens. The rapture of all the love that we have known is His, and to Him belong all the great hopes that have transfigured us, and all the rushing life within which rose again, like Jesus from his grave, when our stricken heart seemed dead. All our joy is God's—we and the Father are one. Praise becomes the air we breathe, and from our praise flows so great a gladness that others learn to praise.

And then, when sorrow comes and pain, we are not unprepared. We know they are in His order whom we love, in whom we are, with whom we are at one. We suffer, but it is with the certainty that the suffering will come to an end, and that the end will be the blessing of others, and, in that, our own. The storm of trial beats upon us, but we are founded on a rock; and there is something almost of joy in the stern resistance we can give to the tempest—such resistance, and such a thrill, as a great lighthouse, set far out at sea on a solitary rock, might feel, were it alive, when all the ocean wrath dashed against it, always in vain. Victory is the only solace for sorrow, and of victory he is secure who with Jesus knows that he is at one with the Father. "Who shall separate us from the love of Christ? Shall tribulation, or distress, or persecution, or famine, or nakedness, or peril, or sword? Nay, in all these things we are more than conquerors through him that loved us."

"More than conquerors." Yet, we have many days of battle to endure, of weakness, and of pain that seems to grasp the hand of death. They have but cold hearts who say that the surety of conquest should carry us beyond the pain of earth. It cannot do so always, nor is it well it should. We must know suffering that we may be able to help those who suffer; we must weep our day, even though we are going to find peace, that we may know how nobly others before us have endured and wrought.

Now are we left without the help of our belief in God at one with us, in the midst of the days when trouble makes praise unnatural. For, if we are at one with Him, then we tell Him of all our trials, as a child runs to tell his mother of his pain. We do not ask Him to take them away from us, but we do ask Him to share them with us. It is not praise, but it is prayer—silent, contending, deep communion, absolute realization of His Presence, certainty of His love, fearlessness, and knowledge; till, at last, we come out of the obscure wood of trouble saying to ourselves, with greater trust than before, "I and My Father are one."

In these experiences, lastly, are the roots of Growth. Through pleasure and pain thus known, and passed through with God, the personal life of the soul develops in such a manner, that while it loses its selfishness in God, it gains the immortal individuality which is only found in love. The deepest personality of man is in his unity with God. Never did Jesus feel more profoundly the undying continuity of his consciousness than when he said—" I and my Father are one."

At last, death comes—death, that men think they fear, but who is our kindest friend. And when we stand before the gate, the key of which he keeps, and see through its lattice his solemn and beautiful face, alit with the light of life—for, in truth, he whom we call death is our nearest image on earth of life—what shall we say to him, with what words unlock the gate of Paradise?—" Open, friend : I and my Father are one."

[June 21, 1885.]

THE UNITY OF GOD AND MAN.

"I and my Father are one."—JOHN x. 30.

THIS wonderful word of Jesus, spoken by him in lofty prophetic feeling of the whole race of man whom he felt moving in himself, lays deep the foundation of all religion. In each one of us growing into the power of truly saying it, personal religion consists. To know our kinship to God, to claim it, to live by it, to love Him as at one with ourselves as a father with a child, to feel that He is educating us day by day into unity with Himself, to believe that the union shall at last be perfect, and to realize it more and more in feeling and in act—that is individual religion. In that relation we each stand utterly alone with God. At times we are conscious of nothing else in the whole universe but ourselves and Him; and this consciousness, and the fact which answers to it—that God has a distinct relation to each of us—different for ever from that which He has to anyone else—is the only unchangeable and certain ground of that which we call individuality. And profoundly important it is to maintain that ground now, at a time when we are called on to sacrifice all individuality for the sake of the whole. We *are* to sacrifice all desires to have, and take, and keep, for ourselves. These are to be surrendered for the sake of the whole. But we are not to sacrifice individuality. In fact, we cannot sacrifice it if we would. If we give it up, we give up the power of sacrifice, for we give up will, character, and consciousness: the very things which constitute our separate individuality. What have we then left to sacrifice? Indeed, the logical conclusion to which certain philosophers, who hold this theory, are driven, is personal and universal annihilation; for if all the individualities of which the whole of humanity is made up are sacrificed, why, then, the whole is itself destroyed. Such philosophies, however, are transient; they must run their course and die, having fractured their heads against human nature and the laws by which mankind exists. No, the religion of Jesus, in which distinctive personality is secured by connecting each human being separately with God, is right, is in accordance with fact, is not only good philosophy, but also common sense. Let each one of you say, "I and my Father are one," and realize towards Him your personality. You can lose personality as much as you like towards man; but keep it towards God. In Him it is certain not to end in selfishness.

Again, if God be at one with each of the parts, He is more completely at one with the whole—or, rather, the whole of mankind is a more complete representation of God than any one of the parts. If each of us may say with Jesus, "I and my Father are one," still more may the whole of mankind, realizing its oneness, say, "I, Universal Humanity, and the Father are one; God and mankind are one." This is the truth which has been kept alive in the doctrine of the union of God and man in Jesus. The form given to it by the Churches is untrue, and most clearly seen as such in the restriction of its truth to Jesus alone: for we may always take it for granted that a spiritual statement issued in a limited form is untrue so far as it is limited. But through the untrue form the truth stole into the hearts of men, awakened their emotions, and produced life and act accordant to it throughout the ages. Of all great social movements, of all great religious reformations, of all the thoughts that have stirred the souls of nations, of all the universal ideas which have coursed like fire through the heart of man, this truth was the living soul—Humanity and God are one. And the day will come, when, after infinite work, struggle and development, victory over all evil error will be won, and all mankind, from beginning to end, will become conscious that it is at union with God, and take up with universal voice, the saying of Jesus—"I and the Father are one."

I showed last Sunday what—on the ground of this belief in our indestructible kinship to God—our personal religion was to be, and in what it consisted.

To-day I will speak of the other side of religion as it flows from this same idea of the kinship of God and man; that side of it which is in relation to our fellow-men. It is an enormous subject. The sermons of a lifetime would scarcely discuss half the forms it takes; and I have spoken of it in many ways. But, however numerous its forms, they all flow from this one idea of the natural union of God with man, of the natural kinship of the Father to His children. For in that idea is declared the truth of the brotherhood of man. If all are God's children, all are bound together for eternity, and have the eternal duties and the eternal rights or fraternity laid upon them. All religious life then, conceived of as lived in and among men, runs back to God as its centre. The idea of the Fatherhood of God is the most ideal and the most practical ground of all human association, from the relations of the family to those of the whole of mankind. All other grounds are liable to change, are contained in the ever shifting matter of human thought and feeling, are capable of being discussed, differed from, overthrown. This alone, being outside humanity and yet within it, being immutable, infinite, and always good, remains a foundation that cannot be shaken. There is nothing which any old philosophy or new religion has striven to embody concerning the duties of man to man, concerning the rights of man, concerning the evolution and the progress of the race, which is not to be best derived and worked from the idea that all men are brothers because they are the sons of the infinite Goodness, Truth, and Love; that all men and the Father are one.

But among the many ways of treating the subject of the religious duties of man to man, on the ground of this belief on which I am dwelling, there is one which is but rarely touched, and which, if I can manage to express it, will develop, in perhaps a new fashion, the belief itself, and the duties that flow from it.

If Nature could consciously feel and speak, it would say, "I and my Creator are one;" and at least, men have so felt and written about Nature that part of the thinking of man is this—"That the universe is one of the forms of God." If, then, humanity and Nature are both forms of God, there is a relationship of kinship, and of essential thought between them. In what Nature does, or in what is done in her, we should find an image of our true lives ; in the doings of natural things, the image of what should be our doings one to another. This, too, was the conception of Jesus. He used continually the processes of Nature, the business of the sun and wind and flowers and corn, to illustrate the Kingdom of God among men. He saw, that is, the inner harmony of thought between humanity and Nature, because he saw that their one and single source was God his Father.

Our question, then, which we wish to answer is : What does the life of Nature tell us of our religious duties towards men? I shall state this in poetical form, but it will be seen that it may also be stated in scientific form.

We see first individuality ; each separate thing living its own distinct life, having its own distinct qualities, and yet, in all, and forming all, only one Energy; different atomic arrangements producing different developments, but the mighty power which drives the vibrations for ever constant and the same. Or, to say the same thing in the poet's way—Out of herself Nature furnishes to every creature a silent heart ; every lonely dell and every mountain peak, every flower, every stream and cloud has its own special soul and character. The vast divisions of the world—the sea, the heavens, the air, the all-receiving earth, like the great divisions of humanity, have each their complex life and personality. And Nature herself, in whom all the separate lives are merged into one life—as persons, societies, nations, and divisions are enfolded in the one life of humanity—

has her own mighty Being which loves, thinks and acts in incessant creation.

But this individuality of the whole and the parts is consistent with, and indeed endures through ceaseless intercommunion, every part giving and receiving all it has, like friends in loving intercourse; each sacrificing—to use an analogical term—its life for the life of the rest. Nothing in Nature lives to itself, or dies to itself. Each bears the other's burdens, and so fulfils the law of God. They do it, I suppose I must say, unconsciously, but they do it, and they reveal to us in their doing of it what God desires our life with one another to become. It is one of His universal thoughts of life which we see there; and the whole statement I have made, as a poet would make it, is just as true, when stated in another form, in the world of scientific fact. It is an absolute truth.

Individual as we are to be then towards God, we are to be the exact converse towards our fellow men. Among men, our religion is to be (and in this we follow Nature as well as Jesus), the surrender of all we have and are for the sake of others, for the sake of the welfare of the whole. We are to possess a blessed spirit in our being which shall yield, almost without consciousness of giving, with joy and without weariness, as a flower yields its scent and a stream its music, whatever beauty and use we have for the increase of the happiness of man, till at last we feel, through our giving, that we are in communion with the whole of humanity. Then we say, "I and humanity are one;" and since humanity is the child of God, say again, and in a different way than before, "I and the Father are one." This is a part of our religion towards man; and he who is not living by this idea, is, so far, isolated not only from God and man, but also from Nature; at variance not only with theology, but also with science; not living in harmony with truth.

Again, as with us, so with Nature, there is a mighty sorrow. The whole creation groaneth and travaileth. Many have looked on the world, and seen in it nothing but pain and destruction. It seems sometimes to us as if the universe were sentient, and we heard the cry of its vast suffering rising in the dead of night, and vainly asking us for help. And did Nature feel, we should know that she would be like humanity, and would realize the same immense trouble that we have, and the same immense problem we try to solve.

But this problem both for her and for us is contained in the categorical imperative which demands the sacrifice of individual desires for the welfare of the whole. As long as we are unwilling to make this sacrifice, so long we shall have pain. As long as humanity is unwilling to obey the law by which the life of the spiritual and the physical universe exists, so long will pain be the lot of humanity. Pain is the unwilling sacrifice of our individual desires to get and to keep things for ourselves alone. Pleasure is the willing surrender for the good of the whole of all things which we should otherwise desire to get and keep. And the only answer to the problem of the suffering earth and man is in the belief, that when all have attained the full power of living for the welfare of the whole, and of using that power with ease, then pain must cease, for that which produced the pain will then produce pleasure. And if so, the end will be so glorious, and the life so intense, that we shall confess that to gain it was worth all the pain.

But now, face to face with the pain, what does Nature teach us? It teaches us to take it joyfully. It is impossible not to be impressed through Nature with the sense of the frank enjoyment of life in organic things; though we know also that all these things suffer the same natural pains that we endure; the animals consciously, and, it may be, even the plants that do not tell us of their woes. Yet they take misfortune well. It was not out of Wordsworth's soul alone that the idea came that every flower enjoyed the air it breathed. Even when we are gloomiest we think how gaily the leaves dance in the sunlight, how happily the stream is running, how wild with pleasure is the mountain grass tossing in the wind. The birds, the insect world, the fishes that flash in the river, the lambs in the dappled orchard—with what gladness without care, themselves their own enjoyment, they live and move, and seem to praise the Lord.

This ought to be a part of our religion towards our fellow-men; yes, in spite of pain, even because of pain. The very first demand on our self-sacrifice, when we are in heavy trouble, is not to let it overcome us so far as to take away the possibility of our rejoicing when its agony is over; and this demand is made on us for the sake of our fellow-men. There is nothing more selfish, more disagreeable, or which causes more trouble and want of love in the end, than the temper of those persons who, because they think their grief a duty, or their trial greater than any one else can know, impose their sorrow and pain upon mankind, refuse all the sunlight of life, and wear the air of incessant martyrdom, without the quiet or the joy of the martyrs. This is incarnate selfishness; and Nature, who suffers enough, protests against it in her silent way of practice. Think how after winter she bursts into life again; think how after tempest the flowers lift their heads; think how after the earthquake and the eruption she clothes the slopes of lava and the torn earth with her green and embroidered garment. Hear how the birds, while they remember their desolated nests, give themselves up to the sweet present! In all this it is the voice of God you hear, the thought of God you see—your Father who is at one with Nature and with you.

What Nature does, midst of all her pain, let us go and do likewise midst of a suffering world. As the flowers do not know the pleasure that they give to the weary and the sick and the poor; as the birds never think how many of that human race so different from theirs have, by their song, been led away from pain or cheered in sadness; so the heart that will not yield to trouble, and in its faith and love keeps and gives brightness, as it ought; which sings on its way, though it does not forget its sorrow—as sorrowful, yet always rejoicing—does more for men than we can tell, and far more than many who consciously sacrifice themselves. These valiant hearts do not know the pleasure and the strength they give, but it is great; they may even, like the birds to us, give comfort to a higher race in greater trouble than we, for all the universe of life is bound together. If you will keep joy in the midst of trouble, you may truly say, "I and the Father are one."

Lastly; beneath all the outward pleasure and pain of Nature there is peace. Deep calm is at her heart, as in the depths of ocean; as in the silence of the starry space. Even greater than the impressions of sacrifice and joy which she gives to us, is the impression of repose, as if that were the end both of joy and sorrow. Yet it is not a dead peace, but one of life at harmony with itself, of laws fulfilled and loved, of soft swiftness of Being, at rest through its own swiftness. The calm of the summer landscape, the quiet of the sea, the tranquillity of the evening, the silence of the night, do not bring to us the thought of death, but of obedient and peaceful life. And this, which might be called mere imagination, is the sentence also of great philosophy and of science. In the higher region of thought where all disturbance is seen in its relation to the whole, where order is seated on its throne supreme, there is eternal peace. In the centre of the universe, there is not death but life; not sleep but energy. It is this tranquil being in the whole and in each thing which "sends its own deep quiet to restore our hearts." It is this unity of energy and rest which, in its last expression, is God with whom we and Nature are one.

So, that is the end. Peace in swiftness of life; rest in fulness of being; harmony in completeness.

Carry that faith with you through all your doings with your fellow-men. You will then carry with you infinite blessing. What Nature tells you, make a part of your religious life with men. Lead them to see and know the end, the end that Jesus knew when he said, "Come, all ye that are weary and heavy laden, and I will give you rest." Infinite peace in infinite life is God. In that also—and it is dear to our outwearied lives—we and the Father are one.

[July 2, 1882.]

THE WANDERING SHEEP.

"What man of you having an hundred sheep, if he lose one fo them, doth not leave the ninety and nine in the wilderness and go after that which is lost until he find it?

"And when he hath found it, he layeth it on his shoulders rejoicing."—St. Luke xv. 4, 5.

There is all the sweetness of common religion in this parable. Everyone can feel it, understand it, love it. It belongs to no creed but the creed of human love; it enshrines no doctrine but the doctrine which we learn by many a gracious touch of God, the doctrine of heavenly pity. It does not lead us into the thorny wood of polemics to find there a faith by which we may live and die; it places us in the midst of simple human life, and tells us that therein we may know religion. Men ask, Where shall I find teaching that I care for; where a daily word spoken to my heart; where the short lessons which, teaching more than sermons, flit like swallows over the plains of the soul, and drop a seed to fructify hereafter into a harvest of perfect good? And the answer is, Open your eyes and look round about you. See the son returning penitent to his father's door, hesitating to enter. But listen for a moment, what do you hear? A cry of joy—"This, my son, was dead, and is alive again, was lost and is found." It is a revelation of God's fatherhood. Take up a common flower as you go over the meadows, the daisy, star of the grass. Look at the way in which the pink is dropped upon its leaves, touch by touch, till you fail to see the gradations. Look how its yellow wands are set in the midst, each with its golden crown. What is that? It is that infinite care of God which Christ knew when he said, "If God so clothe the grass of the field, which to-day is, and to-morrow is cast into the oven, how much more shall He clothe you, O ye of little faith."

Watch the growth of the corn, from seed to harvest. What do you see there? You see the growth of the soul. Jesus knew its story well, and taught his happiest spiritual lessons from all that he saw in the green fields round Gennesaret. Pass by an orchard in spring: you see a tree laden with foliage. Pass by the same orchard in autumn: you see the tree producing no fruit, but only leaves. What does the owner do? He waits a little. Year by year he digs about the tree, and takes care that it has plenty of refreshing nutriment; but if nothing comes of it he says, "Cut it down; why cumbereth it the ground?" What have you seen? You have seen the way in which God deals with a soul whose life produces leaves but no fruit.

Pass by on a Yorkshire moor or Highland mountain side when eve is falling dark and menacing, and the snow comes up hidden in the bosom of the cloud; stay till you see the ninety-nine sheep penned in the rough fold beneath the shelter of the rock, and then, amid the blinding drift, go with the shepherd all night long from glen to glen, till at last he find the dying lamb, and, laying it on his shoulders, brings it back rejoicing. What have you seen? Only a shepherd and his sheep, and danger faced, and joy born out of the depths of love and pity for one of lower by one of higher race? More, more than that. You have seen Christianity, seen the relation of the Great Shepherd to the race of men. The whole world is a parable of the dealings of God with man. The interpretation is plain to all who will open their eyes to see. All our religion, all that is necessary for us to believe may be found in our daily life with men, and can be learnt from the relation of men to animals.

Christ teaches us in this parable to be pitiful to the lost. There are two classes of open sinners—those who go away wilfully, and those who are lost through error. Lost! Mark the word; for it makes the distinction between this parable and that of the Prodigal Son. The fault of severance from a father had been wilfully made by the younger son. Then, he ruined himself of his own direct will; he was not betrayed, or deceived into evil, or overtaken in a fault. He chose the wild life of his own accord. He was not only ruined; he was, we are told, dead. But the wandering sheep was led away, it knew not how, from the guarded flock. A patch of greener grass had attracted it; and then another, and another; a belt of shadow next beside a brook, beneath a tree, had lured its thirst and then its slumber. It awoke in mist and solitude, and in dumb pain and ghastly fear went blindly through the wilderness and was lost. It is thus that many a vain, weak, and passionate creature has perished. The light that leads astray seems often at first to be light from heaven. The frailty which leads them to sin takes often the semblance of strength. The path on which they walk appears so beautiful that it cannot, they think, be wrong. Alas! no mistake is so common as to think that the beautiful is necessarily the true.

Many of these wandering creatures, both men and women, fell in the way of Christ. He was attracted by them, and had himself an irresistible attraction for the outcasts of society. The Pharisee, at their sight, drew round him the cloak of sanctimonious indignation; a touch from a sinner was a stain. The Sadducee did not care about saving them from ruin. He would say, "A certain amount of immorality is inevitable; sin to some temperaments is almost a necessity: I can do nothing, and I do not particularly care; and after all, as there is no life after death, they may as well follow their nature. If they hurt society in following their nature, society can put an end to them."

Between these two sides—which I have modernized a little, and you may recognize their existence now—the publican and the sinner in Judæa were abandoned to themselves. No voice of love reached them; no chance was given them. Reprobated by one side, ignored by the other, they felt themselves infamous, and they became still more that which society declared them to be. Hardness of heart corrupted the strong among them; despair of heart corrupted the weak.

But when pure humanity lived on earth, and they saw the love of God shining in the Saviour's eyes, and shining upon them, and heard in every word he spoke the infinite yearning of God to seek and save the lost, they could not resist the heavenly magnetism. "Then drew near all the publicans and sinners for to hear him." The hard heart melted into tears; the despairing saw the star of hope arise. In the very presence of their foes they clustered round Jesus. But they were not allowed their last chance. Even now the lying righteousness of men forbad their penitence, and pushed them back into their guilt. The Scribes and Pharisees did their wicked best to make the only man who had ever seemed to care for these outcasts turn away from them in shame. They "murmured, saying, This man receiveth sinners, and eateth with them."

What would the prophet do? What would you have done? Would ridicule or fear overcome Jesus? Would he bend before the power of the priesthood, and turn away from the sinful woman and the degraded man? Having opened to them a glimpse of heaven, would he push them back into a hell darker for the glimpse of light? These questions ran through all hearts in the crowd; and I can imagine the suspended hush when Christ began to speak. But can we fancy the shame and anger, the shame and, perhaps, the repentance, which stole into the obstinate Pharisaic hearts: the beautiful relief, the delight, the glory of tearful love which filled the sinners' soul when, one after another, in exquisitely simple words and human images, the three parables which follow fell like musical winds, born in the highest heavens of tenderness, upon their ears? Nothing like those parables had ever been heard before; nothing like them will be heard again on earth. They have come down to us from that ancient time, and they have never ceased to touch, and soften, and redeem the heart of the lost. They have drawn more healing tears from men; comforted more despair; fallen like April rain upon more exhausted hearts; blessed more death beds with the supreme beauty of hope; told us more of heavenly love than all the poetry, art, and religious teaching of thousands of years.

And how was this wonder wrought? By an appeal to doctrine; by an appeal to abstract principles; by an appeal to social economy? Nothing of the kind. By an appeal to ordinary human nature, and to its affections.

He turned round upon the Pharisees, and went direct to the human centre of pity in their hearts, taking the case into a region unconfused by any conventional and hardened thought. "What man of you, having a hundred sheep, if he lose one of them, doth not leave the ninety and nine in the wilderness and go after that which was lost, until he find it?" That is, he asked the objector, "How would one of you act in such a case? You would go after the wanderer until you found it." It is just so, said Christ, that God would act. Think of your feelings when the prodigal returns. These are God's feelings when a sinner turns to Him.

This is simple teaching, utterly simple; a child can comprehend it, a wise man can love it with all his heart. There is no need to represent Christianity as a difficult thing to understand. In the minuter details of life, in the application of the principles of Jesus to diverse characters, difficulties arise. But one simple idea lies at the root of all Christ's teaching—the salvation of the lost, the bringing of rest to the weary and sorrowful and sinful of the world. Broadly and clearly, Christ declared in these parables the identity of God's compassion with our compassion; the identity of God's eagerness to find the lost with our eagerness to find them. It is the fashion with some to deny this identity and to quote "My ways are not your ways, nor my thoughts as your thoughts." Very true! But those words were spoken to men who were sinning by injustice and unpitifulness against true human nature. They did not deny that fact which made the manifestation of God's character in Christ possible and valuable, the fact contained in the phrase of the human heart of God. It is that fact which the Pharisee, at all times of the world's history, denies. Secluding himself in his religious doctrine and formalism, in bigotry and bitterness, he refuses to give love to the sinner, to feel pity for the penitent. It is his religion to be hard on others. He denies his human heart, and though he thinks he affirms God in so doing, he in fact denies God. To turn and believe that God feels love and pity, and is just, not cruel, is the only chance such a man has to redeem his soul. By appealing to the human nature in these obstinate Jews, Christ recalled them from the region of dead and bigoted religion, swept them for a moment out of their world of thorny maxims of morality, of separation from mankind, and brought them back to Nature. Nor does he forget now in his perfect life those whom he touched with so subtle and so gentle a finger here on earth. Wherever there is the wanderer and the sinner there is One who seeks them. We, untempted and folded in the watchful precincts of home, do not know the agony of such loss as this; but there are times even for us when the heart is outcast and the life undone; when broken down with the unutterable pang of a lost love or a fruitless indignation, we hide our sorrow from the eyes of men, and move among them with no sign of outward trouble, but inwardly are wandering for ever through a misty wilderness, wild and thirsty as the most passionate desert dream. Worse still, when, seized in the grip of some secret sin, though seeming righteous to the world, we know that we are no longer of the ninety and nine just ones who need no repentance, but are adrift upon the sea of self-contempt, alone with the torture of remorse and hopelessness and shame. In these and other cases, if we are not spiritually dead, there is but one longing in the soul—the longing or some divine comforter to come after us and say, "Your hidden grief is mine, my child, your secret sin I forgive and forget. Neither do I condemn thee; go and sin no more."

Far worse, however, is the outcasts' case. Thousands of outcasts drift through this great city; women who have sinned, men who have never heard a word of kindness from their birth. They are the hundredth sheep. If you can, be to them, when they cross your path, like Christ and God; do not stand apart; help to save a few from the terror of despair and the death in life. Your own peace, your gracious home purity should make you pitiful. Have you never asked yourself how much you may have indirectly done to swell those dreadful ranks, how thoughtlessness again and again repeated in matters that pertain to every-day existence may have driven many into this outcast life. "We know not what we do," some cry; but they ought to know. They ought to think that more evils are wrought by want of thought than by want of heart, and that thoughtlessness, encouraged or unchecked, or long protracted after warnings given, becomes want of heart. The impulse of pity is checked by selfishness; the desire of helping by vanity and love of show, by disinclination to break in upon our easy going life. The practice of love is troublesome, and at last divine charity dies. Then we are dead to God, dead far more than the miserable outcast we ignore. For death to love is death to God. "For those who shut out love, in turn shall be shut out from love, and on her threshold lie, howling in outer darkness."

Let us open, then, when we can, a door for the broken and contrite heart. We can go after the lost sheep until we find it; we can be untiring in our effort, unsparing of our wealth. For even though we may often fail, we shall resemble that ever-seeking Father, whose children we ought to be in the sleeplessness of our tenderness, and the obstinacy of our assistance.

Lastly, in those words, "until he find it," we see that which I have elsewhere called the pertinacity of God. Human love is baffled by fate; worn by time; exhausted by indifference; made base by fear; tainted by caprice; reversed by a swift circumstance. But the love of God to every son of man moves always true, steady, and persistent to its goal—the salvation and perfection of the soul. He will never cease to pursue the wanderer until He find him. By impulses of soul and sense; by unvoiced words heard in the silence of the hills or in the dead of night; by the sudden kindling of aspirations; by the joy of youth; by success in life; by every divine touch of human feeling; by sudden recollections falling upon us, He seeks us in youth; and, if we will not hear, then He seeks us in a sterner way by the later discipline of life. He makes that seeking felt in trial, in exhaustion of excitement, so that joy itself is pain because it has satiety. He seeks us in the storm which lays waste the garden of life; in the voiceless agony of the soul; in the bitterness of hope delayed; in the darkness out of which we cry, "My God, my God, why hast Thou forsaken me?" For if joy will not do anything for us, perhaps pain may. There is something awful, when we are its subjects, in this terrible pertinacity of God; awful in its trial hours; awful at every hour, when we stop in the midst of joy, to think, "I am haunted by the Eternal God. It is no use my contending against Him—He will make me His at last."

It is awful, but not terrifying, when we yield ourselves to it. It produces no slavish, coward, superstitious fear; nay, it exalts the soul of him who believes it, makes him proud of his destiny, and sends him forth armed, "to strive, to seek, to find, and not to yield." Faith in the perseverance of God is the training which makes heroic hearts. It makes us not only heroic, but also joyful, when we believe in this divine perseverance not for ourselves alone, but for men. Every wandering sheep the Shepherd will seek until he find it. The flock shall be perfect in the end. All shall be brought home on his shoulders, rejoicing; the perseverance of the Charity of God shall look at last upon the whole of mankind folded in the embrace of heaven.

This is the work of God. Do what you can in it to make it complete, if I may use the word. Go after and seek for those that are lost, and in the end you shall have joy and reward. What reward? Material good, a comfortable place in heaven! Oh, not that, but a sure and exquisite reward, if you have the heart to feel it. The fruit of love is love. You will have the manifold growth of tenderness within your soul, the divine pleasure of saving the lost, the same delight that filled the heart of Christ when the outcast and the sinner gathered round him. You will have something more: you will realize the sympathy of heaven with your work on earth. Listen to the exquisite and beautiful touch in which this thought is held. "Likewise I say to you, there is joy in the presence of the angels of God over one sinner that repenteth." I pray that the music of that thought may thrill in your hearts and kindle your love, while you walk hand in hand through life with Jesus.

[Nov. 5, 1882.]

ETERNAL PUNISHMENT.

"Be not deceived; God is not mocked; for whatsoever a man soweth, that shall he also reap.

"For he that soweth to the flesh shall of the flesh reap corruption; but he that soweth to the Spirit shall of the Spirit reap life everlasting."
—GALATIANS vi. 7, 8.

IT is now many years ago since a partial victory was won in the English Church over the doctrine of eternal punishment. It was plainly declared that to hope for universal redemption was not inconsistent with subscription to its formularies. I remember well with what joy this tiny boon was accepted by many of us. Since that time, the revolt against the doctrine has been going on in a great number of the orthodox religious bodies. Even among the Wesleyan Methodists—perhaps the most strong of all the dissenting sects in their assertion of eternal punishment—a disturbance has arisen which has greatly afflicted the leaders of that body. In England, in Scotland, in the Church of Ireland, this subject has been so prominently brought forward, that many ministers have ceased to declare directly the doctrine of eternal punishment. And now an ever-increasing number of the clergy, and a still greater number of the laity, have wholly and openly put out of their creed this abominable opinion.

To those who worship in this chapel it is scarcely necessary for me to speak upon the subject; but it is important that I should try and put into as clear form as I can the arguments against this doctrine, in order that they who do not believe it may be well armed to contend against those who do, and to help on the cause of God by overthrowing it.

To this position men have come but slowly. To say that the doctrine ought to have been held abominable a century ago, would be absurd. The mass of men cannot be before their age, and the doctrine of eternal hell could not strike the religious men of the past as immoral. Neither their idea of God nor their idea of man fought against it. Men did not believe then in the universal brotherhood of man, and, therefore, could not believe in the universal Fatherhood of God. But from the moment that in the political and social sphere of thought the idea of mankind as one nation of which all men were, by right of their manhood, citizens, and of all men as forming a universal brotherhood, took shape and ran like fire over the world, kindling the commonest soul into passion—the doctrine of universal redemption began to grow in the minds of men. Religious men, arguing from what they felt as citizens, conceived a loftier notion of the duties of God's Kingship. He owed it to Himself, they felt, to redeem, and ennoble, and make perfect His subjects. And arguing from what they felt as brothers one of another, they felt that in the realm of religion universal brotherhood could only be spiritually based on a doctrine of God's universal Fatherhood. If, then, God is the Father of all men, and men His children, it is incredible that a Father can send to utter moral ruin and eternal pain the greater part of His children. If He does, He cannot be a Father; He has no sense of the duty of a Father, nor of the love of a Father. If eternal hell be true, we have no God at all, or none we choose to worship. And the declaration through Christ of God's Fatherhood is the cynical mockery of a tyrant.

That kind of argument took root in this country first through means of the poets, who feel more strongly than other men the duties and necessities of the heart. Then it stole into the mind of the laity, and, lastly, it reached the clergy, and it will not be long, though it lingers among the natural conservatives of the Church of Christ, before the old doctrine perish out of every pulpit in the land, and the test of orthodoxy be no longer—" Do you believe in the devil?" but this—" Do you believe in God the Father?"

The doctrine of eternal punishment ought to be denied, because of its evil fruits. A good tree does not bring forth corrupt fruit, and we owe to this doctrine all the slaughter and cruelty done by alternately triumphant sects in the name of God. It gave birth to the Inquisition; it drove the Jews to unutterable misery; it burnt thousands of innocent men and women for witchcraft; it tortured and rent the bodies and souls of men; it depopulated fertile lands; it ruined nations; it kept the world for centuries in darkness; held back civilization; and in all ages urged on the dogs of cruelty and fanaticism to their accursed hunting.

So dreadful were its deeds, that a door of escape was provided from its full horror by the Church of the time. The doctrine of purgatory and of prayers for the dead was the reaction from its terrors, and it saved religion. Unrelieved by this merciful interposition, eternal punishment would have slain the world.

Those were its fruits in the past, and on this account we ought to deny its truth. But now we ought to fight against its lies day by day; for we who do not believe it have no notion of the harm it is doing to those who do believe it. We are bound to contend against it if we have any desire that a nobler Christianity should prevail among men, for its teaching drives men into violent atheism. The less educated classes, who yet feel strongly, and perhaps more strongly than the educated, the things of the conscience and the heart, say that it denies all their moral instincts. And so it does. It makes them look on God as an unreasoning and capricious tyrant, and they turn from Him with dread and hate. It makes them consider the story of redemption as either a weak effort on the part of an incapable God to save man, or a mockery by Him of His creatures on the plea of a love which they see as derisive, and a justice which they see as favouritism. And till we free the teaching of Christianity from this doctrine, religious teachers will still continue to give, as they do now, the greatest impulse to infidelity among the working classes, an impulse much greater than any given by all the materialism of philosophers, or all the attacks of iconoclasts.

As to its influence on educated men, it is this. It throws an air of fiction over the whole of Christian teaching. These men cannot believe it if they believe in God. It represents, even apart from God, no idea at all to their minds. They know, being accustomed to reasoning, that the idea of everlasting punishment is inconceivable. But they are told that it is bound up with the whole of Christian doctrine; that if they do not believe it they cannot believe the rest. They do not like to openly leave their Church or sect, and to profess themselves unbelievers; they are thus driven to a mere conventional assent; till, by degrees, Christianity (infected in their minds by this false doctrine) drops altogether out of their heart as a life-impelling power. They see what they believe to be a fiction walking about unchallenged and unreproved among doctrines which, unaccompanied by this traitor, they could receive as honest and true, but which, bound up with it, they must reject. And, sooner or later, they do reject the whole. The one black sheep has infected all the flock, and all the flock are slain.

It has as evil a result in the case of those who teach it—and, indeed, in the case of those who are silent about it but accept it—for it makes them unconsciously false. Of all who teach it, who believes it? Only a few! The rest think they do, but do not. If they did, it would tell more vitally on their lives. A living faith in any truth influences the whole life, changes character, modifies or rules all our dealings with men; and the belief in eternal goodness has that power. But the belief in eternal evil (for eternal punishment means eternal evil) has scarcely any power over the daily thoughts and acts of men. In more than half the acts and thoughts of those who say they hold it, it is implicitly denied. The greater number of those they meet are damned to eternal torture, to torture endlessly renewed with exquisite skill, so that when countless ages have rolled away, it cannot be said to have begun, and into every moment an eternity of pain is pent; and, believing this of their friends, and relatives, and fellow-men, they can eat and drink peacefully, and beget children for whom that fate is reserved, and move without infinite horror among men. Nonsense! They do not believe it at all. Do you imagine there are a hundred persons in England who believe in eternal evil as they believe in eternal goodness? They might as well know their own minds and say at once, "No! we do not believe it. It has no influence at all on our lives." But that is just what they will not do, and they reap their reward. They sow to lies, and they reap lying within. They think by asserting and asserting to convince themselves and the world of their faith. The world smiles behind its sleeve while they spend half their time in diligently hiding away the fact that they do not believe what they say they do, till all their teaching becomes unreal.

They reap their reward, I say. It is a terrible business to have a falsehood domiciled with truths. It is worse for its possessor, when he is only half convinced, or not at all convinced, of its truth, to take the greatest pains to dress it up like a truth. For the falsehood gets no good from the truths, but the truths all get maimed by the falsehood. These men talk of the love of God, and His mercy, and His pity, and His justice, and His righteousness, and His fatherhood, and the goodness of salvation. All the time they are talking, this hideous companion in their own soul is laughing at all these things. Love of God! What of eternal torture? Righteousness of God! What of eternal evil? Good news, salvation! Fling them to the winds! And this, which goes on often in their own mind, goes on still more in the minds of those who listen, until the trail of a lie and its sickly smell defile their whole religious life. This evil belongs chiefly to the Protestant, less to the Roman Catholic. The latter, at least, is better off. He has a chance, and more than a chance, of escaping this eternal doom.

That is one set of reasons why you should denounce the doctrine of eternal punishment. But those who most strongly assert this doctrine put forward an ethical objection to the opposite doctrine of universal redemption, which is at least worth considering. They say that the denial of the doctrine of eternal punishment produces the greatest of evils, because it destroys the doctrine of retribution, and weakens our fear of doing wrong by taking away the punishment of wrong doing. This is the ethical objection, and it has its weight.

But, in answer, I ask, first, what efficacy has fear in either bringing a man to God or in deterring him from sin? It is not the terror of Christ, but the love of Christ which constraineth us to give up our guilt. The weapon of religious terror is always a devilish weapon, and it drives men to the devil. It confuses and renders idiotic a weak man. It hardens a strong one into fierce rebellion. It drives some to despair or wretchlessness of unclean living; others to scorn or hatred of God; and the sacrifices it makes (unlike those made by a heart broken by love) are the sacrifices that the savage makes to his god, of whose character he is ignorant, or whom he fears because of ignorance.

As to its fruits, what are they worth? The obedience

wrung from a child by the uplifted lash, the reverence given through fear; would that please you, fathers and mothers in this congregation? What would you think it worth? It is selfishness, not obedience! And do you think that God wishes that selfish cry, or that He fancies it obedience? If so, what sort of God is He? Is a God obeyed only through fear worth obeying at all? Is *this* religion, or superstition and idolatry? No, we lose nothing in getting rid of the motive of fear, as the motive of religion.

But, in getting rid of that motive, and in denying the eternity of hell, do we in truth destroy the doctrine of retribution? Not at all—we establish it, and are enabled to assert it on clear and reasonable grounds. First, we can believe in it. The heart and the conscience alike refuse to believe in everlasting punishment. The imagination cannot conceive it. The reason denies its justice; but the retribution taught by the opposite doctrine— That God's punishment is remedial, not final, that it is exacted, but that it ends when it has done its work—is conceivable, is allowed by the heart for its root is love; is agreed to by the conscience for it is felt to be just; is accepted of the reason for it is based on law.

It is only when we deny eternal punishment that we can assert in a way in which it can be believed the doctrine of retribution.

And, in our belief, the ground of retribution is this: That God cannot rest till He has wrought evil out of all spirits, and that this work of His is chiefly done by causing us to suffer the natural consequence of sin. The very root, then, of our belief in the non-eternity of punishment involves an awful idea of punishment. For on this ground God will not cease to be a consuming fire to a man till He has destroyed all his evil. Nor can He cease. The imperative in His nature binds Him to root out evil, and God does His duty by us. Does this view destroy and not rather assert retribution?

We can all understand that. Introduce evil into your life, and you are introducing punishment. God will not rest till He has consumed it. Sow to the flesh, and you will of the flesh reap corruption; you shall eat the fruits of your own devices, and find in them your hell. And God will take care that you do. For His love knows well that only by knowing the bitterness and death of sin, you can be brought to hate it, repent of it and cry, "I will arise and go to my Father." Nor will God spare a single pang, if only He can bring us to His arms at last. Punishment here and in the world to come is no dream, but a dread reality. But it is strictly and justly given, and naturally it comes to a close. One cry of longing repentance changes its quality, one bitter sorrow for wrong, one quick conviction that God is love and wishes our perfection. But to produce that repentance, and till it is produced, God's painful work on our evil is done and will be done.

That is not the work of a tyrant, but of love. It is no weak love, such as we are accused of preaching. It is the mighty, all-knowing love which looks to the end, and in merciless mercy uses the means. It is love according to law; the kind of love of which, when it has wrought its saving work, we acknowledge the justice. It is love which, though it causes suffering, does not injure the heart, for the root of it is not desire to make us suffer, but desire to make us pure, and true, and like the eternal Love which must be true to right or cease to be love. When we have faith in that strong tenderness at the heart of punishment, when we know that every suffering God inflicts on man is born of His desire for their perfection, of His longing to make us all His own, the heart rebels no more against punishment, nor does the conscience. The purified conscience itself claims retribution, will not be content to be let off from punishment—because were that possible, the sanctity of perfect law would suffer, and injury done to it would injure the whole world. The more ennobled the moral sense of man becomes, the more does he insist, even to his own pain, on retribution. That which I have sowed, he says, I must reap.

Then you may say, "What chance has a man of escaping in the end, if he is bound in this way under law." No *chance* at all! Things in God's world are not chance! No chance, but certainty of escape, according to law. When he ceases to sow weeds he ceases to reap weeds; when he roots up the useless, poisonous plants in his soul and burns them, then the soul receives the good seed, nourishes it, and he brings forth good fruit. Then he is no longer in punishment, retribution has become reward; but both are terms for the one thing, the one law—That what we sow we reap. By the same law we are in pain or in pleasure, in hell or in heaven, according as we use the law. Surely that is plain enough, sensible enough—the answer of the conscience to it is unhesitating in approval; the answer of the scientific reason is as clear in its approval.

But, some say, this change is not possible hereafter, man's character is fixed at death—as the tree falls, so it lies—they that are filthy are filthy still. The results of a long life of sin can never be destroyed or altered. Habits once rooted have a tendency to continue, and when the change of death comes, we enter into a state in which these evil habits have unrestricted room to develop themselves, and do so.

First, that is nonsense. The analogy of nature is against it. A tract of the earth may have got into a habit of earthquakes, but the upheaving force exhausts itself, and then nature repairs her wrongs, and the desert of lava becomes a fruitful field. An evil climate has slowly degraded a species. But if the climate change, the animals gain new powers, seizing and appropriating what is useful for their development. But these are only analogies. The facts are against this brutal theory. I have known men who have been idle for years become hard workers under a new impulse, and those who have been under the power of habits of evil, such as seize on body, and soul, and spirit, overcome those habits and become new men; and if that happens even once, the single example refutes this theory, if we assume a God of love who is working with incessant impulses upon human souls.

"But He does not work so hereafter," they say, "in the world to come." There is the real point, then, and what have we to say of it?

It asserts either God's powerlessness to redeem the guilty or His unwillingness to do so; the first assertion is treason to Him, and the second blasphemy. If God cannot save, what becomes of His omnipotence? If God will not save, what becomes of His love? And if love be violated, what becomes of His justice? In the acid of this theory God is utterly dissolved.

"No," it is said, "sin is justly punished with eternal ruin," because, done against an infinite God, it is itself infinite, and, therefore, requires infinite punishment. That is a statement which catches the understanding in a trap and persuades it that it is satisfied by a show of logic, by a clink of words; and it has had in times past, and even now, a certain charm and attraction about it for many persons, such as a riddle has, or a trick of words which always seems on the point of being discovered, but never is discovered, because it cannot be discovered. And thousands have lived and died believing it. I do not blame them in the past. The idea of God was built up on the idea of a despotic king. But I do blame, and severely, those who believe it now—because the higher light has come, and they shut their eyes to it. No one now thinks that might makes right, and yet, some men still continue to impute that wickedness to God. Moreover, what does the theory really assert? It asserts not only eternal punishment, it asserts eternal evil. It gives to evil the essential ground of the nature of the Deity, and makes two eternal powers in the universe, and these two for ever in opposition. It makes absolute goodness contentedly or uncontentedly permit absolute evil. It strips God of omnipotence, for it is wholly impossible to conceive —without destroying the very nature of goodness—that it has the power to destroy evil and does not exercise it. God cannot allow eternal evil and continue God. And if He allows eternal punishment, He does allow eternal evil. It is a vile conception, and if it were true, we should be forced to pray to a cruel power for the only favour we could with all our hearts desire for the world and for ourselves, the favour of instant and complete annihilation.

But lastly, it is said, that if eternal punishment be not true, neither is eternal blessedness. They stand and fall together, and if we destroy the belief in everlasting punishment we destroy the belief in everlasting happiness. That statement also sounds well. But what does it really mean? Translate it into clear words, and its falseness at once appears. Eternal punishment asserts eternal evil, as eternal happiness asserts eternal goodness, and then the statement is actually this: If eternal evil be not true, neither is eternal goodness. And that is not only blasphemy but folly. Goodness, if there is an everlasting God, is naturally eternal, self-existent, without beginning and without end. And the heart and reason of mankind accept that statement. It is on that ground, of the natural and essential everlastingness of goodness, that we believe in the naturalness and necessity of everlasting happiness for those who are good at death, or become good after it.

On the other hand, everlasting misery is neither natural, necessary, nor possible, just because evil is not necessarily eternal. That is not eternal which has an origin, and evil had a beginning; that is not eternal which is not self-existent and absolute, and evil is neither one nor the other, unless we say that evil is in God. The eternity of good does not involve the eternity of evil. On the contrary, it implicitly denies it. The argument is all the other way. If everlasting happiness be true, it means everlasting goodness; and if everlasting goodness be true, it means that evil cannot be everlasting; and if evil be not everlasting, punishment cannot be everlasting.

But, after all, what should we need of argument, if men would listen to the God within their own hearts. Ask those whose hearts are pure, who hate evil with the same passion with which they love God, whether they have ever conceived of the possibility of eternal sin except in connection with a sense of disbelief in God, or at least have ever felt that the answer of their own heart—in moments when it was most consciously filled with God—to the question, Is evil eternal? came as clearly as the answer to the question, Is good eternal?

When we think of the eternity of sin, life is accursed, shrouded in unmixed and fatal gloom. The world is hopeless, its vice and sorrow bound on it for ever, and eternity, even if we are saved, stained and blackened with unfading horror; and God Himself, our King, an unrelenting tyrant who either cannot or will not conquer sin. We are told that God has conquered the evil of the lost, because He has trampled them down for ever and ever into hell. That is not conquest, but rather the notion which a savage chieftain has of conquest. It only subdues the outward powers, and leaves within the heart of millions, still burning unsubdued, the unconquerable will to do wrong, the "study of revenge, immortal hate, and courage never to submit or yield, and what is else not to be overcome."

But when we think of the eternity of goodness and its

victory—and this we have now been driven to—the soul exults, even the blood stirs with joy ; all nature seems to sing along with us. Life puts on its noble aspect. In our loneliness high thoughts and hope are our companions ; among the crowd of men the light, and life, and joy of God move along with us. All work is dignified and great. Things seem worth the doing, thoughts worth thinking, endeavours worth perseverance, temptations worth resisting, trials worth the toil of conquering them, life, even the commonest, worth living nobly to the end. The curse of time departs. We can behold all the energy of decay, but can still rejoice. We know that God, who made all things fair, lives, and will live for ever till He has made decay into life, and all the things that failed as fair as their ideal—for His goodness is infinite in the accomplishment of beauty.

And the wild sorrow of the world, tossing like a midnight sea its uplifted waves to heaven in supplication ; and our own sorrow and the passions which rend and consume the heart, each an atom of dark water in that sea of sorrow; and the vice, and crime, and selfish greed which make of earth and of our own personal life so ghastly and so drear a thing when our eyes pierce beneath the sugared crust on which we pace so merrily, as if there were no rottenness beneath—there is but one truth which can obliterate the horror of that vision, which can enable us to fight against wrong, and to conquer in the end, and give us power, faith, and hope in face of this awful revelation. It is the unconquerable goodness of God, the conviction, deep rooted as the mountains, of His infinite love and justice, the knowledge that the world is redeemed, the victory over evil won, and that though the work is slow, not one soul shall be lost for ever. For he shall reign till He hath subdued all things to Himself in the willingness of happy obedience, and the joy of creative Love.

[July, 1882.]

THE COMMUNION OF SAINTS.

"Wherefore seeing we also are compassed about with so great a cloud of witnesses, let us lay aside every weight, and the sin which doth so easily beset us, and let us run with patience the race that is set before us.

"Looking unto Jesus, the author and finisher of our faith."— HEBREWS xii. 1, 2.

THE Christian Church has for many generations set apart a day for the observance of the Feast of All Saints; and its eve, celebrated in poetry, in games, by wild and graceful superstitions, and bearing in its practices traces of heathen faiths and legend, has been called All-Hallows-Eve. The Feast was originally set up to put an end to the excessive multiplication of Saints' Days. These grew so rapidly—each nation wishing to honour its own special saints—that more than half the days in each month were turned into holidays. Work was neglected, and laziness seemed in danger of developing into a virtue. The Roman Church, then, while it wished to preserve reverence for these lesser saints, wished also to end the scandal, and threw the veneration and love of all these holy persons into one festival instead of many, and the day was called the Feast of All Saints. The term included not only the lesser but the greater saints as well; all were celebrated together;

and the festival finally became the poetic form in which the doctrine of the Communion of Saints was enshrined.

That idea—the inter-communion of all who were holy—was one of the root ideas of the society formed by Jesus Christ; and no greater idea, nor one more original at the time, has ever been put forward in this world. It was the first great international conception. It made a country of which Greek and Jew and Roman and Oriental and Barbarian were all citizens, and in brotherhood with one another. Distinctions of race and character, of caste and rank, of language and learning, were held to perish before the idea of this society, and the only difference among its members was that made by more or less of holiness and love and faith. It conceived, then—though still but partially—of a universal humanity.

Nor was it content to include only those living on earth. It took into its infinite embrace the saintly dead. Time and space disappeared, and the communion of spiritual life and love was established with all those who, from the beginning of the world, had been loving and holy, and who now were alive in God. The meanest slave in a Roman noble's household, the stone cutter who wrought for a scanty wage on the quays of Corinth, was in vital communion—if he were a child of God—with Adam and Enoch, David and Isaiah, with millions of uncounted witnesses for truth who were watching with sympathy and loving kindness their difficult and lowly life. In that vast assemblage in earth and heaven of men and women there was not one trace of death. What prevailed and filled the infinite circles of those who had passed from earth was keen and unquenchable life, and the life was the expression of their eternal love. This was the invisible, as that was the visible Church and both were one assemblage. One spirit was theirs one faith, one country, one home, one humanity, one brotherhood, and one Father.

And among, and for ever with this host on earth and in heaven, was Jesus, their master, leader, and inspiring friend, the captain of their salvation; him in whom the ideal of their human nature had been realized, author and finisher of human love and faith and holiness, whose spirit ran like living fire through them all, and whom they loved with love which could endure all things rather than be false to the life he had lived before them, and to the ideas and passions that inspired it. They had in him the human centre of their communion, and the host in heaven and the host on earth were one in him.

But this was not enough. There was still needed an eternal, immutable, absolute centre of life and love and power, in whom and by whom the whole assemblage might consist, and be for ever secure of continuance and of development; from whom life and love and holiness, unfailing, increasing, and joyful, might for ever be outpoured; so that progress might be certain, and bliss in it undying. And this was God, their Father, the ground of all association on earth and in heaven, the binding power of the whole, the centre of this Rose every petal of which lodged a thousand thousand souls; radiating His light and life and love and might to every human heart, and in the unity of this spiritual effluence binding them all to Himself and to one another.

This was the full idea of the early Christian Church, and it was unique in the history of religion. But no great idea remains in the form it has originally taken. It develops with the further development of mankind, and this idea, long kept back from growth by being bound up with false or limiting opinions, has, since the outburst of more universal ideas concerning humanity—an outburst of which its unconscious working was the cause—taken a fresh expansion. It is no longer limited to certain sects, or visible churches, or religious castes. It embraces all mankind. It says that because God is the Father of all men, that therefore this communion of saints will be co-extensive in the end with the whole race—that all will be brought into holiness, all live with the life of God, all be filled with the same love and faith with which Jesus was filled. The Communion of Saints will finally be identical with the Communion of all Humanity. This is the final form which, in the belief of all, this conception will assume, and its power as an established faith will change, exalt, and govern the whole world.

The Positivist idea of humanity is but one inadequate form of this idea; inadequate because it has no absolute centre outside of humanity; inadequate because it is more or less bound up with the opinion of the death and annihilation of every human being; and degrading, not so much because it is accompanied by death and not by life, but because it keeps up the idea of a kind of hell, that is, of a class who are sacrificed for the sake of a few, who are useless to others save as warning, and unable to live in the memory or in the lives of men. Nevertheless, as it does declare a communion of noble men, independent of national and caste differences, it is useful, and so far will live. But it only lives as an offshoot of the original thought, and by the life of that thought. It is essentially a limited conception.

Our idea is far different. It conceives, first, of the whole of the righteous and loving beings of the past as now living in God, for one another, and for those on earth, and ever moving forward into loftier life and work. It conceives of all those in the past who have died while yet unrighteous and unloving as also moving forward into holiness and love, until they join the great assemblage of the just made perfect; until they also, beginning a redeemed and noble life, shall feel vibrating through them the loving spirit of this vast communion.

It conceives, secondly, of the present human beings abiding on this earth as living also in God, the holy, consciously, the unholy unconsciously; but both indestructibly bound up with the humanity of the past, watched by it, helped by it, and hour by hour passing onwards into nearer union with it.

It conceives, thirdly, of the whole mass of beings that shall hereafter live upon the earth as conditionally held in this communion, fated to play their part in it, and finally to complete that numberless nation of humanity which shall take its part among the other forms of spiritual being in the peopled universe of God—a perfect race.

And through all the past humanity, through the present, and through the thought of the future humanity which lies still unfolded in the creative thought of God, one thing for ever moves and thrills—infinite, universal life. One quality for ever grows—it is holiness. One passion for ever burns an unquenchable fire, and makes life for ever kindle into fresh joy, and holiness for ever quicken into fresh work—the passion of that love, which, flowing forth from God, fills and irradiates the universe.

This is the idea, and it is only with a quiet smile that one who possesses and is possessed by it can receive the invitation to change it for any offered to him by the new religions. I should not change the pearl of great price for an imitation pearl; not the music of the spheres for a discussion on its existence; and I will not change all mankind alive in God for all mankind dead in dying knowledge? To catch and keep the best Thought—that should be our struggle, and when we have got it and love it, he is a fool indeed who does not cling to it.

And the more we cling to this conception and love it, the greater becomes its power over life. It becomes a ruling portion of that faith by which we daily live. At first, only a little of it is doubtfully believed; the full splendour of the truth only unveils itself to long and mingled work and contemplation—work, not done on it as an idea, for that would bring us into the thorny wood of theology, and finally to the caves of vanity or of despair; but done for men, and among them, for the sake of the truth you have learnt, and inspired by the joy of the idea—and contemplation of it, not as an abstract thought, but of it as it takes form in the lives of men, of its power as seen in our own use of it.

As we use it thus, and thus contemplate it, it will develop itself in us and before us; add to itself within us the glories it always possesses without us in the mind of God; until it may be granted us, before we die, to see it in all its fulness. That is the progress of all great truths in the soul of those who love their light. They seem at first like the thin clear sickle of pale and trembling light which, seen through dim mist, we call the moon, but which, night after night, grows fuller, till at last in death we behold it rounded, perfect—apparent Queen of all the sky.

That is belief in the communion of humanity in God, and no time is enough to tell of its results on the inward and outward life. They vary in every soul that believes the truth, being conditioned by the soil in which it grows. But there are some of these results which vary little, and among them are certain truths which most console human life. These are the best to speak of now; for the world is very weary and sad in these days. It needs no rough treatment, but consolation.

The first is that this faith tells us that we are never alone. The very ground of it is that in the midst of this vast world of Being, supporting its existence and pervading it, touching it at all points, and conscious of the life of every soul in it, is God, our Father, at once the vital principle by which each several being—to borrow an illustration from science—spins on its individual poles, and the æther in which independently it moves. He knows every thought; He feels every sorrow and every joy; He supports with all the force of law every effort towards goodness, that is, towards union with the eternal in the universe; He makes us feel, when we are in evil thought or act, our contradiction to the whole universe, our apartness from Him; till at last, we yield ourselves to goodness only, and are consciously at one with Him.

It is a joy so great, that all the sorrows and pains of life may well be borne to attain it. It is a life so vivid, so unspeakable, that the whole universe of nature, and the whole past, present, and future of humanity seem to live within us. We are ourselves, and yet we are all nature, all mankind. And the paradox is true, that at the very moment when we have lost personality in the whole, we are most conscious of the rapture of life. If, even after many, many years, that should be true, and true it will be, there is no greater comfort possible to man. For it means the very absolute of perfect joy in the midst of perfect goodness and perfect love.

And, secondly, it is not only God who, according to this idea, is present with us for solace and for power, but also all the noble dead—all who live in God, and who, through the unity of His pervading spirit, are interwoven with us in the infinite web of immortal communion. Their lives are mixed with ours. Their personal sympathy, joy, love, and comfort are communicated to us. "Lo, I am with you alway, even to the end of the world" was no foolish saying. "I will not leave you comfortless, I will come to you," was no mere fanciful expression. Jesus knew this truth, and knew what he would be able to do. And what he said as man, all men who believe as he believed this truth may also say, when dying, to those they leave behind. We, too, can whisper with a smile to our friends and our loved ones when we are going away—"Lo, I am with you always;" "I will not leave you orphaned of my presence, I will come to you." And we shall be able to do that very thing. Yes, we who are struggling here are not left alone by the dead who are alive. Not only God, but our own humankind are with us, in vital communion, sympathizing like God with all our good, sorrowing for all our sin, and helping us in all our trouble. Jesus is the lover of our soul, and so are all the holy and loving souls who live in the eternal world. He is the nearest, and the most conquering in his love and in his communion. But yet there are some whom we have known and loved on earth who have to us a relationship of union, not so powerful in love, but nearer in human bonds. These are ours, and the tie between us, though they are not seen, is closer even than it was on earth. What is its ground, where is its strength rooted? In the truth of the Communion of Saints.

Finally, there are two things more to say—One is, that all the joy and comfort of this doctrine depend on our becoming pure in heart, holy in word and deed. We cannot believe in a Communion of Saints until we are becoming saintly. All the glorious forms which the idea takes, all its evolution into higher and higher forms, are destroyed in us by evil doing and evil thinking. The first and foremost way to gain belief in it—the gate into its splendour—is the struggle to gain righteousness. It is an idea then that bears on conduct; and it unfolds itself to holiness. If you want it, if you desire its consolation and its joy, live hour by hour to gain a pure and loving heart.

Communion with God is known through holiness. The pure in heart see God. Communion with humanity in God is known by Love. And there is no other way in the world by which we can believe in God and believe in Man.

And, secondly; when we think of this vast assemblage, all united in a **communion of** saintliness, **we understand** that the last and highest range of human nature is not knowledge or power, but holiness held in love. It is a thought we would do well to recall in the midst of **this modern life of ours.** Here, power, wealth, intellect are first. There, it is different. Power dies, disarmed by **goodness;** isolated wealth **has no** place in the celestial country where all **have** equal welfare; knowledge passes away, lost in love **which** sees what knowledge vainly strives to find. And the one thing which **is** eternal, which is the root of true power over men, which is the true wealth because it possesses the good and joy of all things, which is the ground of all true knowledge, which develops out of **itself** faith and hope and love—is goodness. The goodness of **God is the centre of** the universe.

[April 1, 1883.]

ATONEMENT.

"And I, if I be lifted up from the earth, will draw all men unto me."—ST. JOHN xii. 32.

IT is a strange phrase, this glorification of death. For death in itself is vile, and men shrink from its presence. It seems to be the remover of power, the destroyer of love, the depriver of thought. We bury out of our sight, with the same natural dismay, the dead king of men and the dead clown, the dead poet and the dead fool, the face that thrilled a nation and the brutalized features of the savage. "As the one dieth, so dieth the other, so that a man hath no pre-eminence over a beast; for all this is vanity." What is death but horror and hatefulness?

But no man, not even the materialist, believes that this is the whole account of the matter. It is not death which is attractive or repulsive, but the spirit in which men die, or the thoughts awakened in us by their death. The death of a selfish man has all the hatefulness of death; but the thoughts awakened when a noble and loving character has passed away draw us continually round his memory. We love him in death, because he is alive in us, an inspiring and quickening power; we are drawn to him because his life makes us hope that the world is better than it seems. And around his grave cluster all those feelings which soften the heart as April showers the grass dried by the winds of March. Regret, love, ennobling sorrow, sympathy with all who loved him, delight that he has been so good, yet pain that so much is lost to us, faith that he is giving now of his good to others, spring up and flower and bear fruit in us. We are softened and inspired; the life we lead is made more delicate in the midst of a world whose ways are dusty and whose temper is hard. Being lifted up from earth he draws men after him.

But the main thing which attracts us is not so much the thoughts and feelings which are awakened in us, as the spirit in which a great and loving man meets death. The surrender of life for the sake of truth in defence of an idea necessary for mankind; the conscious sacrifice of worldly honour and of wealth for the sake of others, the conquest of pain and fear by the love of man—this is the attractive power of the cross. It is the one thing which has in all ages been beautiful to men beyond all other beautiful things.

Men have given a fleeting worship to power in war or power in intellect, but they have given adoration to Self-sacrifice. It is not to Cæsar, but to Washington that we turn when our hearts bestow the crown of glory on the rulers of men. It is not around the brilliant intellect of the selfish genius that our love and reverence approach to worship, but round the prison bed of Socrates. The spirit of the cross of Christ still and for ever attracts the soul. "If I be lifted up, I will draw all men to me." There is but one supreme beauty—the beauty of perfect love; and it wins the enduring love of men. "I, if I be lifted up, will draw all men to me." It wins also the love of God—"Therefore doth my Father love me, because I lay down my life for the sheep." This, then, is the attractiveness of the cross; this is the reason why all nations have come to pour out their love beneath its shadow! For all the varied and partial manifestations of this annihilation of self through love of truth and love of mankind were concentrated in the life and death of Jesus Christ.

But the beauty and the attractiveness of the cross are not confined to Calvary. The spirit of the cross lives in men, and wherever it is found it does its work. It draws us out of evil by its loveliness, and when we are convinced of its beauty, we rise out of spiritual death. It happens sometimes that we are tempted to be careless about truths, to hold moral convictions slightly, to drift away from our early love of a life above the common standard of the world. We are then in the general stream of things, and our weakness or our desires lead us to go with the current. Now and then, led by a higher impulse, we contend for a little time; but at last, after many failures, we think of resistance no longer, and our life becomes trivial, mean or thoughtless. Effort will not at first redeem us. Only a great admiration, only the vision of a great spiritual beauty will kindle us into that fire of love which will give effort power. And one day we meet a man who, through evil report and good report, has been true to convictions, who has lost much for truth's sake, whom the world has not conquered, but who still loves the world; and there comes upon us a new inspiration! We admire and love and become ardent to be like him.

And in the rush of love we take up again the ideals of youth, and are born again into a fresh and noble life.

What has done this? It is the same power as that of Christ's death in the man. It is that he has been enabled to show forth in his life the beauty of the sacrifice Christ put into these words: "For this end was I born, and for this cause came I into the world, to bear witness to the truth." And the loveliness draws us to itself. An atonement with good is wrought for us and in us.

Or, take another example. We are tempted in the midst of comfort to complain of our lot. Without pain, without real trial, one of our rose leaves is crumpled. We magnify a little grain of difficulty, which if we were less troubled with prosperity would weigh lighter than a feather, into a mountain. And it is strange how one little thing, when dwelt on, establishes a power over us, and spoils the whole of life. The veriest trifles seem to ruin some men's lives. Yet it is not the trifles themselves, but our dwelling upon them till we are absorbed in self-consideration, that does the evil work. Nay, sometimes in our prosperity we invent troubles, because our life is monotonous through want of labour, and end by believing our own inventions — so vile does life become without the beauty of sacrifice!

I remember once knowing one of this temper whom God led into friendship with a man who moved serenely and with love among his fellows, and did his work with cheerfulness. To him the complainer entrusted his trifle of trouble, and wearily asked for sympathy. And the sympathy was given, and the remedy suggested, as if the slight thing were really great. And through the sympathy, effort was born; and in the air of effort the rose leaf began to grow smooth again. But still the man remained untouched by love. The result of selfishness lasted, though the cause was removed.

One day, however, he made a discovery. He found out that his friend, whose life seemed so much at rest, whose cheerful activity was so inspiring, was the constant victim of a disease which consumed him with pain; and that the evil lives of other men kept him in ceaseless difficulty. Yet there was no complaint, no word of reproach to God, no remissness in work, no disbelief in men. He loved God, he loved the world, and he was silent concerning his own pain.

Then shame fell upon the slothful complainer, redeeming shame, shame that soon lost itself in wonder and love. A new ideal of human life was born within him; his own life seemed base in the light of this revelation of true beauty, and yet so great was the attractive power of the beauty, that in desire to be at one with it, he forgot his own baseness and pressed forward to imitate it. He was saved from self, and born into the life of love. What was this beauty—what was it which drew him to union with it? It was the loveliness and the power of the cross of Christ in his friend.

Even so now is Christ always redeeming men through other men who are like himself; even so is the true efficacy of all atonement continued through the passing years. Yes, when the passion of self-surrender begins to stir in our hearts, we feel in it the prophecy of all the love and beauty which will follow from it. Its first breath is like the earliest airs of spring, that, flowing through the winds of March, tell of the change and loveliness that are at hand.

Spring has begun in our hearts, and we shall produce leaf and flower and fruit, the harvest of love and righteousness. It is the substance of things hoped for—this first attractive power of sacrifice.

ii. But it is said that Christ's sacrifice of life and love not only attracts to itself, but also redeems us from sin. How is that? Is the statement true?

We will be content to find an explanation, not in mystical interpretations, nor in logical schemes of redemption, but in the doings of our common human nature, in the plain and living facts of human life. The laws which ruled the life of Jesus were the laws which rule the life of all men. That which is called his atonement is no isolated thing, but the central exhibition of an existing law that every day is at work among us; and the law is—That love when revealed creates love, and that love, when it is wholly given for others, redeems from sin those who believe in love by destroying the root of sin, by killing selfishness.

First, then, the sacrifice of Christ, that is the giving up of his whole life in love to mankind, was a revelation to us that God was not anger, or jealousy, or vengeance, or hatred—but love, and love to us; that He did not need to be appeased or bought off, but that He only asked us to be reconciled to Him, and to love Him. And that revelation, when it is believed, saves us from enmity to God. The conviction of love awakes love. "What," we say, "God loves me; then I will love Him!" And to love Him is to love goodness, and to love goodness is to do goodness, and to do goodness is to be saved. We are drawn to God, and in love of Him we are saved.

That is not difficult to understand. It is within all our experience. When our heart is filled in youth with that eager, passionate, all-absorbing feeling for another which men call love, what happens? All life is referred to the person we love, our self is lost, we are delighted to surrender all things; we are wholly at one with whom we love. So it is, in higher fashion, when we love God. We lose ourself in love of our Father, in love of His character, in love of truth, and purity, and perfection. The very root of sin is burnt up in the union of love. Our whole life alters in the passion of aspiration, in the personal delight of growing like to Him. It matters not that the growth is often slow. We know, in loving, that eternal life is begun in us; that the power is now within which must destroy sin in the end.

That is part of atonement—of our reconciliation to God bringing a new life with it; and it has its analogies in our common life. It is natural, easy to be understood, and wholly human.

But there is more. We are reconciled to ourselves; our whole life is changed, and punishment is transmuted. Let me use an old illustration of mine. There was once a widowed mother who had an only son. All her love was lavished on him, her life spent, her work done, entirely for his service; not a moment of the day but was devoted to him. Her love became a common-place to him, and he took it as we take the air we breathe. It even came to weary him. His life became thoughtless, his youth made him cruel. Then he left her alone, and, far away in the great city, wasted her substance in riotous living, till he had spent all her goods. Afterwards she died; but, though neglected, slain indeed by him, her love had remained unbroken. Still hoping for him, still forgiving, her last words were messages of love. The long self-sacrifice was over.

Had it been in vain? Love never is in vain; never faileth.

The son heard of his mother's death, returned to his village, and, in the quiet evening, went to see her grave. Then all came back upon him, her long patience, her unwearied love, his forgetfulness and her remembrance, the beauty of her tenderness, the horror of his ingratitude—and in a moment the careless heart was broken. A spring of love gushed from the rock, and the softening river of penitence began to flow. Hatred of his sin awakened —it was sin against her! Self-loathing stirred, and he was tempted in despair to return to his old life. But then he heard of her last words. They were words of love. She did not despair of him, she believed in him, she forgave; and when he felt that he was still loved, he took a nobler courage than that of despair, and the renewal of his life began. "She shall be alive to me!" he cried. "There is yet time, and I will be worthy of her love. I will be all she wished me once to be. We shall meet again, and I will fall at her feet and say, 'Mother, all your love was not lost; it lived in me, and made me a new creature.'"

And it was true. A mighty love, awakened by love, took him away from self; he thought no more of his own pleasure, but of what hers would be. His whole life was overshadowed by her immanent presence, ruled by her, renewed by her; till, at last, conscious of the wonderful change, he knew that he had been made good, and was reconciled to his own life. He felt sure he was redeemed.

But had he no punishment? Oh yes, redemption of life through the awakening of love for love is not primarily redemption from punishment. Nay, at first it is the giving of punishment. The pain at his heart was keen, so keen that one might almost say the punishment had only now begun. But it was remedial punishment. Born of love, it worked towards the same end as love, the one end towards which all worked now in him: the regeneration of the life through the regeneration of the heart. The pain kept her goodness, truth, and forgiveness continually before his eyes. It stung him into new efforts to be worthy of her; to do for others all that she had done for him. And, at last, through the work it did, it ceased to be felt as punishment. When he became wholly at one with the life he loved, he felt pain no longer. The punishment had lasted till it had ennobled him, till it had wrought in him the peaceable fruits of righteousness. Thus, and thus only, was he redeemed from punishment.

But he *was* at once redeemed from self, from hardness of heart, from inability to feel punishment, from the tendency to yield to temptation, from a base life, from the sins of the past. He was a new man in love—nay, a new man in Christ Jesus, for it was the same love Christ felt, which dwelt in his mother, and wrought upon him.

Is that true or not? Are there not a thousand instances of the same kind occurring in the world around us—friend who so saves a friend, wife who so saves her husband, minister who so saves his people, men who so save a nation? Is that simple, human, natural, easy to be believed, appealing directly to our reason, affections, experience, worthy of all love and reverence, irresistibly attractive? If so, turn and believe in the doctrine of human atonement revealed in the life of Jesus, for that is its inward work, as its outward work is to make us believe that God is love.

It is nothing, I repeat, which Christ alone can do. It is something he did fully and perfectly, and which we all can do, and are bound to do. We can all, in following his life, reveal that God is love, and save men by love. We can all be atoning persons. Put aside all the difficulties the intellect has woven round the doctrine. Do not seek to reduce it to a scheme, do not bind up its beautiful, simple, and natural tenderness in logical propositions. It refuses to be bound. It is infinite, for love is infinite. See it in its human and divine simplicity; do not call it a doctrine, call it a law; see it as the perfect fulfilment of the common law of love, whereby all redeeming, comforting, healing, and blessing work has ever been done on earth and will ever be done in heaven. Then accept it as the law of your life, and you will begin to live. And as you live by it, and in the doing of it, you also will become an atoner in the same way that Christ made atonement. You will know the meaning of being saved by Christ, of being redeemed by his death, of being cleansed from your sins by him, of being made at one with God by him; of fulfilling in your own life his salvation, of being yourself, through him, through dying to self in love, the Saviour of men, the cleanser of them from sin, the atoner of them to God. And as you grow up into him in this life, the beauty that eye hath not seen, nor heart imagined, will be yours. You will know at last in all its meaning, the import of the text—" I, if I be lifted up, will draw all men to me."

[April 8, 1883.]

ATONEMENT.

"Above, when he said, Sacrifice and offering and burnt offerings and offering for sin thou wouldest not, neither had pleasure therein; which are offered by the law;

"Then said he, Lo, I come to do thy will, O God. He taketh away the first that he may establish the second."—HEBREWS x. 8, 9.

IF an innocent man should suffer, what is the common verdict of the world? It says—"There is a crime beneath the seeming innocence, or he would not suffer." That was the judgment of the friends of Job, and the book of Job gives the Old Testament answer to this blind opinion. The complete answer is in the death and suffering of Jesus. It has been written there for all the world to read, that this stupid maxim is wrong. Suffering does *not* always prove God's anger, nor prove the sufferer's sin. If increase of love were possible, never did the Father so deeply love the Son of Man as at the hour of the Cross; if increase of righteousness were possible, never was Jesus more sinless than in that hour of human agony and apparent defeat.

Nevertheless, it is astonishing how strongly this superstitious view of God's anger as manifested in human suffering clings to the minds of men. It has vitiated the whole view taken of the death of Jesus by large numbers of the Church of Christ. They are so unconsciously influenced by the thought that where there is suffering there must be sin, that they ransack heaven and earth for arguments, and violate all the essential ideas of God and man to account for the coincidence of the suffering and of the sinlessness of Jesus. The Cross is suffering: therefore, somewhere about the sufferer there must be sin, and God *must* be angry. But, they say, Christ had no sin; then what does the suffering mean? Their half-pagan maxim puts them into a sad dilemma.

At last, light comes to them—not spiritual, but logical light—and the thing is clear. Man sins, they say: and sin against an infinite Being is infinite, and deserving of infinite punishment. A debate takes place in the nature of God. Justice says —"I must punish, I will take the law." Mercy replies "Have pity." "No," answers Justice, "I must have my bond." Then love steps in—" Is there no way to make Mercy and Justice at one? The Son of God is infinite. Let him bear as man the infinite punishment; let the sins of the race lie upon him; let Justice exact from him the forfeited bond; let God's anger be poured upon his head. Then, Justice being satisfied, Mercy can have her gracious way." And this, they say, was done; and, therefore, the Cross is no exception to their maxim—Where there is suffering, there is God's anger.

I do not say that this theory was consciously elaborated out of the maxim, but it certainly is its child. It wears on its brow the traces of its savage heathen paternity. In itself, it is entirely a work of the mere reasoning faculty, though a special spirituality is curiously claimed for it. There is not a trace of a spiritual intuition in it. The spiritual intuitions are all against it. It outrages the moral sense. If I murdered a man to-morrow, would Justice be satisfied if my brother came forward and offered to be put to death in my stead? It outrages the heart. It makes a father, who is perfect love, pour his wrath upon a guiltless son at the moment when the son in perfect love chose to die for men. It outrages our idea of God. It makes Him satisfied with a fiction. It makes His notion of justice totally different from that which He has given us. It represents the All-Wise as in a painful dilemma, out of which He can only escape by a subterfuge. It divides His nature, setting one part of it in opposition with another—Mercy against Justice—and so destroys all conception of His self-unity.

That theory has, I hope, begun to disappear from amongst us, but it is on the most absolute contradiction of every point of it that we base the doctrine of Atonement. It is well not to lose the word, even at the risk of misunderstanding. The word is a good one, and only needs to be freed from false ideas to express quite clearly true ideas. Christ did *not* come to tell us that God needed to be reconciled to us, but—that we needed to reconcile ourselves to Him; Christ did not come to tell us that God was angry with us in the sense here spoken of, but to deny that; and to reveal to us the very opposite—"That God loved us, and longed for us to love Him, that we might be delivered from our sin." Christ did not come to die for us, the innocent for the guilty, that God's justice might be satisfied, and because of this satisfaction, be enabled to show mercy to us. He came to die that he might make us feel, through the intensity of his human love, how much God loved us, and make us understand that God's justice, though it punished, was final mercy. Christ did not come to tell us that we should be saved if we believed in his righteousness being imputed to us, but that we should be saved if we lived his life; because that life, being the same in kind as God's life of love and goodness, and holding in it the power of righteousness, was incompatible with continued sin. Whosoever lived in that love was saved from sin. Christ did not come to enable God to forgive us, he came to tell us that God had forgiven us. And it is in the revelation of these truths, every one of which is in direct opposition to the propositions set forth by the forensic theory of Atonement, that the good news of Christ consists; it is by the knowledge of these truths, and faith in them, that man is brought nigh to God, induced to love God, made at one with God. And when that divine and blessed work is wrought out perfectly in every man, then will all Atonement be completed, and God and mankind be at one, as Jesus was when he said—"I and my Father are one."

It was to free us then from this false and pagan view of God—that God was to be propitiated by bloody sacrifice of the innocent for the guilty—that Jesus lived and died. It was no wonder, and it is no wonder that men refused to be reconciled to a God whose justice was satisfied by the punishment of the innocent; who created us to sin, and then, being angry with us for sinning, sent us hell; who followed His own caprice in saving or condemning; who had no real love at all for us, only love for His own power and glory; and who remedied the mistake He permitted us to make by a scheme so clumsy and so unjust that it would be rejected as dangerous to morality by any court of law in ancient Rome or in modern Europe. For a parallel to it, we must fall back on the legends of savage nations, who derived their notions of divine law from those superstitious conceptions of the gods which are naturally engendered in the minds of men by that which seemed the terrible caprice of the powers of Nature. And it is a view of God, which, as in the savage it produced all the evils and abominations of pagan worship, so now it produces all the evils and abominations of religious intolerance.

Jesus denied it altogether. He revealed a God of compassion and love, whose life, he said, was in loving all His children. They had sinned, it is true, but God asked them to unite themselves to His righteousness, in order that they might sin no more. No propitiation was required but that which would be wrought in their own hearts when they believed that God was love and came to ask Him to receive them. Men feared God, but Christ said their fear was foolish. God was of that beautiful and heavenly character, tender, just, fatherly, ready to give them all His Being, that, if once they could see Him as He really was, fear would be drowned in exceeding love. And Jesus recorded, in words of eternal loveliness, in the parable of the Prodigal Son, the way in which God felt towards a sinner—the way in which He received a sinner when he came to himself and returned to his Father. Not one word about propitiation, not one word of any condition save that which is contained in the abandonment of a foolish life and the rush of love in the heart which cried, "I will arise and go to my Father"; in the rush of humility and desire to be good which cried, "I have sinned against Heaven and before Thee, and am no more worthy to be called Thy son." Yet God, being righteous, could not abide sin, and He did demand its surrender, and sacrifice for sin. But the sacrifices He asked for were such sacrifices as Jesus made to God, and none other — the sacrifice of pleasure and self-will and wrong for the sake of being like God in character; the sacrifice of life for the sake of the welfare of the human race; the sacrifice of self made day by day for the sake of truth, justice, freedom, of intellectual power, of spiritual progress, for all things and all ideas by which the advance of man in God is promoted and secured. God did not demand the sacrifice of reason, or conscience, or human love, for to sacrifice these things would be to sacrifice God Himself within us—but the giving up and the burning before Him, on the altar of a pure life, of falsehood and shame, of injustice and selfishness, of cruel deeds and words, of impure thoughts and dishonest life, of hatred and jealousy, of heedless pleasure and passion-driven will; of all that made us unworthy of being sons and daughters of the Lord of Righteouness and Love. These were the Christian sacrifices, this the sacrifice Jesus offered to his Father. It is put closely, clearly in the text—" Sacrifice and burnt offering for sin Thou didst not require "; for these were the demands the Pagan thought his gods made of man. Then said I; then said Jesus: "Lo, I come to do Thy will, O God!" He took away the first kind of sacrifice, that he might establish the second.

It is when we believe and trust in such a God that we are atoned to Him. It is because we are saved through our belief in these truths which Jesus revealed, and for which he died, that we say we are saved through him; that we say we pray to God through him. It is not that he has saved us through a vicarious sacrifice—it is that we are saved by means of the revelation that he gave. It is not that Christ, out of his essential divinity, has saved us—that is God's work alone; it is that through following the blessed steps of his most holy life we find we are redeemed from sin and made at one with God. It is not because we *need* a Mediator that we pray to God through him, it is because it is a fact that he has been the Mediator—the medium whereby we have learnt to know the character of God, and are saved by that knowledge. Yes, when God's character is known by us as Jesus knew it, we are reconciled to God. We hate God and fear Him no more. We are ready with joy to become at one with God, as Jesus is at one with Him, and in the same way. How can we hate a Father who is fatherly in all the profound meaning of the word? How can we fear One who, if Jesus be true, is ready to give away His whole Being to us in utter love, who runs to meet us when we come to Him with a joy which is more than we can ask or think; who, if He punishes, does so by law and not by caprice, and whose law of punishment is established for the destruction in us of evil and the perfecting in us of good.

To believe that is to be saved; first, from our own ignorant and ghastly idea of God which sets our whole life and thought and feeling wrong; and secondly, from our sin, because when we know God as He is and love His character, we become that which we love. To love God is to give up sin; nay, more, it is to win a heart which cannot sin, so that the statement of St. John, "He cannot sin because he is born of God," is not so extravagant as it seems. This is Atonement, the reconciliation of man to God, through the knowledge that Jesus has given us of God.

2. But the work done did not end here. The revelation made of the Fatherhood of God—the revelation that He loved all men as His sons—the intense reality into which Jesus threw that revelation by dying for its truth, the mighty belief in the love of God which urged him to love men so much that he died to prove to them that love was all in all, the spirit of that death becoming the attractive force of the world—the one thing which it was worth while to follow—all these things and their related actions entered into men of all nations, tribes, and kindreds and bound them together into one whole. Man became reconciled to man in the love of God revealed in the life and death of Jesus Christ.

Before the time of Jesus there was no bond of union between different peoples, except that of subjection; nay, rather, different nations were natural enemies. After his time, the moment a man became a Christian, he became in idea the brother of all other Christians. The Jew and the Gentile, the Roman and the Greek, the Gaul and the Briton, the barbarian Scythian and the philosopher, the Athenian poet and the Dacian slave, the Roman matron and the poor Syrian woman—one and all, all nations, all castes, all classes of society, all classes of women as well as of men, were united in a common name, in a common nation, in a common citizenship, in a common love to one another and to God, in the man Christ Jesus. It was no fictitious bond, but one made active, charitable, real, in every city and every land where went the story and the gospel of the Lord. Of course, the idea was contradicted again and again in the carrying out of it; that is the fate of all great ideas. It was most contradicted when the Church became imperialized and changed into a system of castes. But, nevertheless, the idea was working on behind the false systems, and it is working now.

The little Church of Christ was the first international society, the first republican brotherhood, the first equality. And all our political struggle towards the conception of one nation, the nation of mankind, in which all citizens are free, equal, and fraternal, not only because of their rights being equal, but because of the equality of the duties which men owe to one another—is but the working out in society and politics of this mighty atonement of nation to nation which Jesus set on foot in the realm of the spirit of man, when He bound the whole of those who believed in his tidings about God into one Church, by a common love of God, by a common following of his own spirit, by a common belief that, since they were sons of God, they were brothers one of another. That glorious work continues, and as the day will come when all shall be at one with God, from the least to the greatest, so the day shall also come when men shall know and love their unity.

That was another part of the work of that which is called

the Atonement, but which may more truly be called the Reconciliation of Man.

3. But there was one hatred which men had, and have now, which it seemed impossible to turn away.

Hatred of suffering in ourselves, in others; hatred of death as the last and bitterest of pains. Pain by itself—independent of reasons why it is to be borne—physical, and still more mental pain, is the hateful thing. Can man ever be reconciled to that? There were two things, however, before the time of Jesus which had made pain seem beautiful. One was Conscience; the other was Love. Men had for centuries —men, too, quite ignorant that what urged them to die was an atomic habit—rejoiced to die for what they thought right and true, for ideas likely to benefit their own people: and they had found in their inward thoughts of right a strange joy which enabled them to overcome or despise the suffering. These were the great souls of the world; but save in war for their native land, it was not supposed that many could or ought to do this. Suffering did not bring this kind of joy to all men.

But Christ declared by his life and death—and it was one of those daring generalizations that lift him so far above all other prophets—that this which had arisen here and there among men, was the highest duty and law of life; that it was to be obeyed and fulfilled, not only by the philosopher and the hero, but by the child, the woman, the common citizen, the slave, the savage. There was not a man or woman who was not capable of this, not one who in this way of suffering for righteousness, or for the sake of ideas useful to men, might not have all the noble calm of the philosopher, and all the splendid joy of the hero. "Blessed are they that are persecuted for righteousness' sake, for theirs is the kingdom of heaven."

Jesus swept the particular motive into the universal. Not for one's own people only, not for one's own class alone, but for the life, honour, and advance of all mankind, even for those who hated us and put us to death, was this sacrifice to be made. It was in this spirit that the Christian, bond or free, endured torture and death for sake of conscience and truth, and finding in himself a reconciliation to all the sufferings he bore, was the means of reconciling other men to suffering. And how wide-spread this reconciliation of men to suffering became is plainly laid before us in history.

Once more; men had, before Jesus, suffered and died for love of others. There is a feeling in the heart—which they, at least, did not know was only an atomic dance—and which we still call love, which since the world began has made animals, and still more men (for it deepens as life grows higher and more complex), not only bear pain, but rejoice in it, if it can save others towards whom that feeling exists. But that passion which illuminated and transfigured suffering was only felt by men and women towards a very few—the small circle of home, or friends whom they distinctly and personally loved. Christ declared that this isolated passion was to be made universal. That which the mother feels for her child when to save it she smiles at pain; that which the lover feels towards his mistress when to free her from trouble, he gladly dies; that same passion which makes pain and death a garden of delight, the veriest

Paradise on earth, the height and depth and burning centre of ineffable life and joy;—Christ felt when he gave up life for love of all mankind, even at the very moment when he also felt the pain most deeply. Nay, it was reached through the extremity of pain.

To feel that we are reconciled to suffering through love of one whom we know and love, is noble: but to extend that to those we know not, nay, to our enemies, because they are sons of God; to have this unutterable passion for mankind, and, in it, unutterable joy in the heart of suffering; is the ideal life which Christ said was possible to all of us—and it is possible. We shall know what it means at last, and when it is known, we shall be wholly reconciled to suffering.

These things, then, which belong to the law of Atonement, are not theological dreams, woven out of the intellect, not parts of a scheme. They are developments of human powers natural to man, things possible to his nature; growing out of the common life of man; ideals, but practicable ideals; the flower, according to law, of plants in the garden of human nature.

Christ manifested these powers, showed that they were practical and possible, made us understand that we could also blossom into this perfection. And that was another way in which he brought salvation to us, took away our sins, and justly earned the title of Redeemer.

His revelation reconciles us to God, reconciles man to man, reconciles man to suffering.

[April 15, 1883.]

ATONEMENT.

"Blessed are the peacemakers: for they shall be called the children of God."—MATTHEW v. 9.

THE relation of man to God, as long as man is unholy, is the relation of a wrongdoer to one who, on repentance, forgives the wrong, but whose forgiveness is not believed in. It is a common condition of things between man and man. We are ready to forgive, but we find that the injurer does not forgive us. The man that does wrong to another is proverbially slow to believe in love, and therefore in forgiveness; nay, often he is set into greater hatred by forgiveness, because he thinks forgiveness is hypocrisy. This is natural enough. For the injurer, being full of hatred and anger, imputes to the injured his own feelings, and realizing their ugliness in the other through imagination, hates them in him, though not in himself, and feels himself wronged by their existence. Two results follow: first, he cannot forgive the state of heart he imagines in the other; secondly, he cannot believe in forgiveness at all.

It is the same between evil men and God, as long as there rankles in their heart suspicion of God's resentment. As long as they imagine God to be altogether such a one as themselves, there is no reconciliation possible.

They will not forgive God, and they cannot receive God's forgiveness. It has no power. Till it is believed, it cannot produce its blessed fruits in the soul. Hence the deep necessity of that on which all religious writers insist, the necessity of faith.

I repeat then, here, in another form, that which I have already said. Two things must take place in our soul before we can feel ourselves at one with God, before Atonement is an inward fact of the spirit. First, we must change our false view of God for a true one; and, secondly, our own character must grow more into harmony with God's character. It was Christ's work to set on foot these two changes. He made clear to us that God was not jealous of us; that He was not vindictive; that He did not play with our weakness; and, therefore, that we had no longer any reason to hate Him or to suspect Him; that it was false to impute to Him, as we had done, the baseness and selfishness of infliction of punishment for the sake of His own glory. And that revelation (when it is seized by the soul as a fact), frees us from all desire to contend against the Father. We cannot be angry with perfect love when we know it as Love. The first step in our own reconciliation to God is made when our false view of God is replaced by the true one.

The second is the direct result of the first. Believing God to be Love, Redemption, Fatherhood, we must become miserable when we separate ourselves from His goodness by doing or thinking evil. The conviction of eternal love melts the soul into penitence. And then the love of Love awakens, and out of penitence we rise with a mighty cry to unite ourselves to Love; and united to Him, we cannot do otherwise than repeat in our lives the righteousness we adore. So our character is changed, and in that change the certainty of our union with God is secured. It is the second part of our reconciliation.

We are then atoned, reconciled to God through Jesus in this sense, that he gave us such a revelation of God's character that when we believed in it we could be angry with God no longer, but were, so to speak, compelled to love Him; and that in so loving perfect goodness, truth, righteousness, purity, and mercy, we grew like that which we loved; and this inward change of heart completed our oneness with God.

And I said that this representation of the doctrine was not apart from human life, was in reality nothing strange or new, but the complete fulfilment in Jesus, and the flowering in him of those acts and spiritual powers by which all men who have reconciled man to man, all who have atoned together nations or societies, have done their atoning work from the beginning. It was nothing more than the fulfilment in a complete life of that law of love and of forgiveness which has prevailed and saved from the very first—the finished manifestation of the principles by which human love has always done redeeming work.

I purpose to-day to show how these principles apply; so that we may carry them out in our own lives and be ourselves atoners—persons who bring together those who are severed one from another; and, as far as single individuals can do such work, persons who unite divided nations; and lastly, persons who so regulate their inward life that they are enabled to bring into atonement within themselves the jarring elements within their heart.

Jesus, then, according to the view I have laid before you, did perfectly for us and for God what loving and true men have always been doing less perfectly for man and God since the beginning of the world. Whenever any man has been loving, forgiving, faithful to justice, he has made, however unconsciously, his brother man feel that God is of the same loving and faithful temper. He has revealed the character of God, and brought men to love it; and, in doing so, has changed the character of men from evil to good. He has wrought an atonement.

It is one of our most benign and blessed works to do this work. We reconcile men to God, when we show forth God in our lives. If we love men, we make men believe that God is Love. They see God in us, and when they realize Him through loving Him in us, they pass onwards into love of Him for Himself alone—and, loving Him, are changed into His image. This is the redeeming, atoning work we all may do, and it represents exactly the atoning work which Christ did in perfection. And this is no mere theological doctrine, but the simple declaration of facts which everyone can see if but the eye is set to look for them. It is at once the explanation and the proof of all Atonement, as we have conceived it.

Again, to extend the parallel, the way of Jesus is the best method we can use, if we wish to be the peacemaker between two men who are at enmity, one of whom has done, and the other of whom has suffered, wrong. First induce the one who has suffered wrong to forgive the other. You will find that the more easy thing to do. Then you will have established a condition partly analogous to that which exists between God and man—forgiveness on one side, wrong on the other. But there is a difficulty, and it is, as I have said, that the doer of the wrong argues from himself to the character of the injured, and imputes to him his own evil passions. He hates and suspects the other, as Saul hated and suspected David, as many men hate and suspect God.

What is your work, then? It is to go to the wrong doer, and to reveal to him the true character and feelings of the man he has injured, his love and his forgiveness. He may not believe this at first, but harden himself in hatred; still, if you persevere in your proof, he will not persevere in his suspicion. And when he yields at last, his character is changed by the revelation, and he himself, becoming noble again, feels that he is forgiven, is, in fact, changed, and the change is his forgiveness. Then he can reknit the old friendship without untruthfulness and without shame. That is a constant occurrence in men's lives. Let some kind expression of one whom we thought an enemy be told us, let us find unexpected love in the heart of a brother, lover, a wife to whom we have done wrong—and our heart warms again. Sorrow awakens, and love resumes its gentle sway. The character of the loving person is told, and the announcement of the character changes the heart of the unloving. The evil is repaired, and life is again happy.

Alas! it is not always possible to make life happy again, even though reconciliation is made. There are wrongs we do which we repent in vain. We are forgiven the wrongs, but we cannot undo them. The forgiver feels them less because he has forgiven, but they have done their work. It is a dreadful thing when, lightly, only for the sake of getting vengeance, we give ourselves up with blind wrath to slander or persecution of another; and it is not so uncommon in this hot-hearted world of ours. We may then discover, all too late, that one whom we have pursued with hate, or with the revenge of love, is still loving to us, still helping us unknown. Then the heart is broken with the late remorse of affection, and the love of our whole life seems too little to express our repentance for the ruin we have worked by our wrong.

It is often too little. We repent our evil bitterly, weave with fruitless tenderness a thousand flowers of kindness round the life we have destroyed, wish to give up the whole world, nay, even to die, if only we may build up again the temple we have shattered so recklessly. It is of little use. The ruin is a ruin still, however we may clothe it with flowers: we never can rebuild it. Our work is done for this life. Only the divine Architect, and only in a happier world, can repair the miserable work our passionate hands have done. Oh take care! Watch against revenge, against jealousy, against hatred. Once they seize the heart, we never can say what their madness may do to men and women. Repentance saves the soul, forgiveness heals half the pain of the forgiver, but neither buy back the past.

That is the extreme case, though it is not uncommon.

But often the wrong can be repaired, and to help men to repair it in the way I have sketched for you, to look out for opportunities for reconciling men, is to do on earth something of the atoning work of Jesus Christ.

ii. But to pass from this to a larger part of the subject. I have said that part of Christ's work was, first, by establishing the love of a common Father among men, to establish the idea of a common Brotherhood, and by these two to do away with the enmities of nations. A spirit was infused into the progress of the world which went on reconciling nation to nation. A mighty conception went through the world, like a great prophet, to make an international atonement.

It partly succeeded, and partly failed. It has succeeded so far, that Christendom recognizes, beneath all its dissensions, its unity in the worship of a common Father. And this has been one of the great civilizing powers of the world. But while this first idea has succeeded, the second has been neglected. The Apostles had scarcely died before the notion of a common brotherhood decayed. Nay, more; men divorced the love of mankind from the love of God, and wars, persecutions, national and religious hatreds, proclaimed that those who worshipped the same God did *not* consider themselves as brothers.

It may be it was necessary, in the slow progress of mankind, that this idea, so far beyond the time at which it was proclaimed, should suffer from reactions which in the end should establish it more firmly; that it should go through all its excesses and all its defects, so that it might be more clearly grasped by men. But nothing is sadder than the long waiting that mankind has yet to go through, before it is convinced that the two ideas of Christ must be re-married before progress is easy and noble. It seems even now almost impossible to make men believe that love to man is as important as love to God; nay, that love to man—for this is the true way to put it—is identical with love to God, and that nations who for the sake of their own honour, as they basely call it, or for their own interest, violate, by war or by oppression, justice or freedom or individuality in other nations, or support those who violate these things, are not worthy of the name of Christ, and live by Pagan, not by Christian thoughts.

What we need now is, that all over the world it should be felt as a first principle, that the sin of sins (against God as against man) is to injure humanity in any of its members; that a war, or a law, or a measure which imposes suffering upon a people (except as the strictly just punishment of crime), or limits their true liberty, or tramples under foot their desire for national individuality, or retards their advance, either now or in the future, is guilt of the deepest dye, is a wrong done to God who has made Himself at one with the cause of man.

It is our work as peacemakers, as a nation that follows Christ; it is our work as individual members of the English nation, to labour to spread far and wide the atoning and reconciling thought that true national religion is this—That each nation should work, not only for its own special interests, or be jealous for its own honour as duellists are jealous, but labour for the interests of other nations more than for its own, and be jealous for the just rights of other nations more than for its own; that nothing should even be done in the present by one nation for its own interests which might in the future put into jeopardy the freedom, the advance, or the individuality of another nation; that, in one word, all that we call so falsely national glory, which means making our military power to conquer respected, should be subordinated to the true glory, which means making our power to do and support the right and just thing loved; that all that we call national prosperity and pre-eminence must be systematically subordinated—and this should be the foundation of all foreign politics—to the interest of the whole of mankind. Till that is done, our Christianity may be personal, but it is not national; and till it is done, we shall never have our rights in the only way worth having them; we shall never gain our true interests, nor realize our true honour. It is only half Christianity to worship God revealed in Christ. We must add to it the service of mankind in Christ.

It is in your power to do a great deal towards that noble consummation. It is in your power, year by year (for year by year such questions rise in English politics), to support by voice and writing, in society, at home, and in your business, the view which regulates our policy abroad on the moral grounds of justice, of love of freedom, of hatred of oppression, of hatred of grasping wars and grasping trade, and to decry and abhor the selfishness and the petty frenzies which, under the cry of England's honour, hide the principles and the passions of the duellist and the savage.

The desire to get more, or the desire to keep what we have unjustly won, is the very antagonist of the spirit of

Christ; the source of all hatred, and cruelty, and violence; the source of nine-tenths of the wars and wickedness of the world. It is as evil in nations as it is in men. Have the heart, as members of a great nation, to live in the spirit of Christ Jesus. To give away, to think little of self, to care for the whole, to love and to die for the great things of justice, freedom, love, pity, progress—that is to be the maker of peace, one of the great atoning band who shall at last see all nations atoned together, bound together by mutual self-surrender into the mighty and glorious Humanity that Jesus shall present to God when the harvest of the world is ripe.

iii. Nor, lastly, is this atoning work which the spirit that follows the life of Christ does in the outward world, less powerful in the inward world of our own heart. There it also sets things at one, there it reconciles jarring elements. The love which loses itself in God, in duty, in man, in nature; the willing offering up of life on the altar which the will, led by love of God and man, builds with fervour in the heart—this is the atoning of inward discord, the reconciliation, the peace, the power that redeems, that raises us within from death.

Look at the world of our own heart! What a universe! where—as it were in a space infinite to thought—we see all human history reproduced. There are as many nations of thoughts within us as there are nations of passions and powers; and they abide in conditions similar to those of the nations of the world; sometimes despotically overthrown under the tyranny of one passion; sometimes all the rest ruled by the unholy alliance of a few; sometimes all independent, or all savage; sometimes in a state of armed neutrality, often all at war, or on the point of war. There is no peace, no atonement in our soul. That which we would, we do not; that which we would not, that we do. The noble ideal struggles with the selfish pleasure; the religious emotion with the scorn of the understanding; swift passion with steady duty; the present fear with the future hope; the desire of the good things of the world with truth to our aspirations; the nobler with the lower being. Nay, more, we often do not know, in our anarchy within, whether we are good or bad, so strangely do the passions and powers glide out of noble into ignoble forms. Love slips into lust, justice into uncharitableness, courage into boasting or reckless display, modesty into fear, love of truth into Pharisaism, indignation into revenge, faith into superstition, love of work into diseased desire of fame, love of rest into sloth, imagination into sensuality, love of clear thinking into suppression of the instincts of the spirit; or the very opposite takes place, and these evil things suddenly become good things. This is anarchy, the state of savagery when every village within is ready at a moment to go to war with its neighbour village.

What can make these warring things at one; bring peace to this little universe; supply the spell by which these conflicting powers can be harmonized towards an aim which God would approve, and which His love shall confirm into a holy unity?

Only one thing; to possess one ruling idea, beyond our self, which all that is within us should obey; to love that idea, and will it, wholly; and, with that, to love God who gives the idea, and is at its root, so that in the end we lose ourselves in God. This idea is the ruling thought of Christ's life—I am the son of God, and God's will I must do. "My meat and drink is to do my Father's will, and to finish His work. I can do nothing of myself. The works that I do, I do not of myself, the Father that dwelleth in me, He doeth the works." God's will recognized as righteous, loved because it is love to man, made the Lord and Master of the heart—that is the reconciliation of the warring elements of the human soul.

Then your whole being will have the peace that Christ had within, and in the same way. When one aim is dominant, and one belief—the belief that you are here to do a special work for God, and not for yourself—the aim, one and undivided, to do that work as God's work—then these two lords of your life will set your whole heart into the peace of order. The aim, being noble, will so ennoble all your passions and powers, that they will not slip into sin or into degradation; the belief, being one and divine, will order all your powers under it into one phalanx of soldiers for a single work. Every human faculty, rejoicing in union each with each, will pass onwards together in a progress which has its close only in the infinitude of God Himself. The soul has peace in this unity—a peace that passeth understanding. The spirit of Christ's life has made all things at one within.

There is yet another thing to say. The same spirit, the spirit which loses itself in love, reconciles us to the sufferings of life, and brings peace to the storms that suffering makes within.

There are some who have suffered vile and grievous wrong. Added to the wrong, there is the sense of the injustice of God gnawing at the heart. So feels many a betrayed woman, many a cheated man. There is but one way by which such a life may find peace. It is the way of Christ. It is by a mighty effort to forgive the injurer. It is to say out of a divine power, " Father, forgive him ; Father, forgive her ; they knew not what they did." It is strange, yet not so strange, so god-like is our nature, what peace that brings, how life is softened and made possible to live again, and how, in some inexplicable way, the sense of God's injustice passes out of sight, for we are at one with God through our forgiveness.

> " Oh, blest are they
> Whose sorrow rather is to suffer wrong
> Than to do wrong."

All evil things that disturb—the rough judgments of the world, the whips and scorns of time, the bitter poison of self-blame, the pain of our desire for revenge, the pain of the wrong itself—cannot live in the sweet clear air of the life of those who, in Christ's strength on Calvary, pass at last in perfect peace "into that pure and unknown world of Love, where injury cannot come." Nay, more, such a heart is reconciled to pain. It feels the nobility it has reached through pain conquered by forgiveness. It says to itself, "It was well that I suffered, for now I am at one with God."

Others cannot so easily win content. They forgive men and gain the peace that comes through forgiveness ; but they are restless still. Their nature is unpeaceful as a mountain stream, which, never to be charmed to gentleness, runs among rocks, and only rests for moments in obscure pools —a rest wilder even than its trouble. Perhaps, in this life, they never can reach peace of heart. Yes ; there are some —not the wicked, but those overwrought by phantasy—who live unrested, and will die unrested, to whom it seems as if eternity itself could not give rest ; on whose tombs might be written, "Without hope, I implore peace." There are more of such men than we know. We may not be of that strange and difficult temper, but in all our lives there are times when this experience is ours; when nervous excitement, fierce pain, base injustice, continued anxiety, decaying love that corrupts the life, the vulture claw and beak of jealousy, ingratitude's sharp tooth—that both of them turn the heart to carrion, and then rend and devour it—have made us hate life and death equally as vile, and send forth from our heart an unutterable cry for peace.

What then is our help? How then shall we reconcile ourselves to life?

Only by throwing ourselves, as Christ did when troubles of this kind came upon him, out of ourselves into love of God, and into love of man. Again and again, when Jesus was half broken-hearted with the evil which attacked him, he went into the wilderness or to the mountain top to pray alone, to realize his union with the Father. In the very last and bitterest sorrow, when even his best beloved could not watch with him for one hour, he sought in the olive garden communion with his Father. And there, in utter loss of self, he found the peace which carried him through a death inflicted by those who hated him who died for them in love.

This is one secret of victory over suffering—loss of self in love of God.

But that alone would not have been enough for Jesus. For such solitary communion tends to isolate us with ourselves. Jesus, and we with him, must lose himself in communion with God through work of love done to mankind. He passed from his own trouble into active help, and forgot all pain in the larger thoughts of what he might do to heal and succour pain. I think some of us might try that way. Trouble, anxiety, discontent double themselves by brooding on them; they lessen to a shred when we seek the anxious, the troubled, and the discontented, and lift them up, using our pain to help their pain. It is by work of this kind that the vast conception of mankind growing through sorrow and sacrifice into union with God slowly arises in us, and dwarfs in the end all our personal distress. We live then in so glorious an idea that we feel our life glorious. We prize the breath we share with human kind, however painfully we draw it; and at last, driven by pain to feel with the pain of the world, learn the ineffable joy of that forgetfulness of self in sympathy with others, which was the support, nay, even the rapture of Christ upon the Cross; which (touched for one moment with the depth of agony) passed into that majestic cry of peace and joy—"It is finished; Father, into Thy hands I commend my spirit."

We may, with him, feel the very worst agony of life, and know we can live no more. But if, in the midst of it, we live in love, if still, for all the pain, we lose ourselves, we shall win the last and crowning joy of death for love. For God does not ask us to live longer than we can. The hour comes when death our friend releases us—and then all our long repression, all the forces of sorrowful effort, all the noble pain, are transformed into the expansion of the soul, into powers of joy, into the inconceivable rapidity with which we live and work in the life and labour of God.

THE LIFE AND CHARACTER OF JOSHUA.

"And Joshua the son of Nun was full of the spirit of wisdom; for Moses had laid his hands upon him: and the children of Israel hearkened unto him, and did as the Lord commanded Moses."—DEUT. xxxiv. 9.

THE education of Joshua is of great interest, and full of lessons to us. It is a long, long time before he steps into the first place. Moses is represented as being eighty years old before he took the lead, and Joshua nearly as old. One thing is quite plain—even though we are unable to consider the history as accurate—that the ancient Hebrews —and certainly the late compiler of the Pentateuch— thought a man who had a great work to do should undergo a long period of training before he entered upon it.

There is infinite care spent on the forming and moulding of the men of genius who are to form and mould the first rude clay of a great people—Greece, or Rome, or England; and the Jew who put these books together makes us conscious of the anxious education given to Joshua through the forty years of the wandering. He held that this was the doing of God, and it is our view. God is at the root of all great nations, chooses and educates specially those who are to represent the type of the nation, and to impress a character upon it. This is what the theologians call election—not the selection, as men have said, of certain to be saved for the glory of God and to the ruin of the rest, but the choice and education of men who are to save others for the glory of mankind, and, therefore, for the glory of God, since God's glory does not consist in damning the world, but in redeeming it.

In one sense we are all elected, each to do a certain part, which no one else could do, of God's great work—the perfecting of the human race. But the true doctrine of election looks rather to the choice by God, and the making by God, of certain great and universal men, who, by their genius, will change the face of the world, create nations, inspire and influence all hearts, embody ideas and make them run like a fire through mankind. It is wonderful the pains God takes with these men: they are "chosen vessels;" and when they die, we look back on their lives, even after a thousand years, and say, "This is the Lord's doing, and it is marvellous in our eyes." That is the true doctrine of election.

Joshua was elected to finish the work of Moses. It was of the first importance that the great ideas of Moses, rude and primitive though they were, concerning God in his relation to the Israelites, and concerning their government, should be clearly handed down and kept; that the whole spirit of the work Moses had done in the wilderness should be continued in Canaan. And we may be sure that part of the endeavour of Moses' life was to secure that this should be done. For that end, he wrought Joshua, and when he died, that work was done. "And Joshua the son of Nun was full of the spirit of wisdom, for Moses had laid his hands upon him."

It was not done in a hurry, but through forty years of companionship, and therefore it lasted. We cannot quickly penetrate a man with our ideas, nor a nation. We are disappointed if our thoughts are not at once as clear to others as they are to ourselves. We are impatient if our children, or those we teach or seek to influence, do not accept, and do not understand our ideas after we have been giving ourselves away to them for a year. Do not trouble yourselves about that. If we believe what we are saying, and if it be true, then, after forty years, we shall have made men who will continue our work, and they will have been worth the making. The followers who are not always worth the making are those who accept us at once; who rush into enthusiasm about us. They receive our seed on ground that has no depth of earth, and when the sun of difficulty comes, their swift excitement withers. In time of temptation they fall away.

Moses made a firm, solid-set man out of his follower. He succeeded because he worked patiently for many years; and he did his work quietly. He let Joshua's union with him grow out of circumstances. It first arose out of Joshua's genius for war. When the infant people met their first enemy, Moses chose Joshua as the leader of the host in battle. It was natural when the battle was won, that Joshua and the Lawgiver should be much thrown together. The thinker must have close at hand his man of action. And we hear that this close relation was established. Day by day, in quiet intercourse, we may imagine then that **Moses trained** the man; not seeking to train **him** specially, **but always** doing it indirectly. And we can well fancy the reverence and love which an unimaginative, plain, unthoughtful, unmystical, **but** fiery nature like Joshua's would have for a subtle, many-sided, spiritual, imaginative, **but** fiery nature like that of Moses. For in fire, and ardour, and courage, they were **equal and at one.** By that reverence and love, growing deeper year by year, Joshua won **the** power of understanding the ideas of Moses, and of rooting them into **his** character. And they were rooted there, and Moses was glad of his work when he died.

But he was not the man to be glad to **have** only a reflection **of** himself, or his thoughts; else he would have **chosen one** who was similar in nature to himself to be his **follower.** On the contrary, he chose a nature entirely different from his own; a man whose genius was **a** genius for war, one who would naturally represent his ideas in a different form, and in whom he himself would see them differently. That was wise, and it proves that **the** one thing Moses cared for was not the form, but the thought; not the temporary clothing of the thought which came from himself, but the Eternal thought itself which came from **God.** It was more than wise, it **was** prophetic. For the thoughts Moses gave the people were to be continued to them in different circumstances. They **had** been given in wandering and in comparative peace. They were to be continued first during incessant war, and then in a national settlement. He took care, therefore, that they should **belong to** a warrior, and be coloured and **moulded in** the mind of a warrior. Nothing could be better for their friendship than

H

this frank acceptance of dissimilarity and its results. Unlike natures, if they love, are kept loving by unlikeness. Each admires and desires that in the other which he does not himself possess. Respect, wonder, and loving curiosity knit them together, till at last each gains and keeps, without losing his own individuality, the good and glory of the other.

That was the friendship of Moses and Joshua—the ground of Joshua's education for his work. And it is full of lessons for us, which I can only indicate. If any one, child, workman, or follower, serve or listen to you, and you have anything to give them, do not neglect them because they are of a different nature to yours, and care for different things. Dissimilarity of nature may be the very thing needed in your follower in order that he may afterwards carry on your thoughts in dissimilar circumstances to those that now surround you. Do not seek to be reflected by those who follow you. It is soothing, but it ruins a man. It pleases his vanity, but as you would not like to have the character which enjoyed posing before a mirror, so you should not like to do the same in matters pertaining to your own thoughts. Your work, always given back to you softened by reflection, will be shut up in admiration of itself; and then—your effort, isolated from the movement of the thought of the world, and from opposition which kindles it into activity—will stagnate and then corrupt. Seek for those to carry on your thoughts who have life in themselves, who will add their own thoughts to yours, and who, while keeping your thoughts, will bring them forth in a new garb, and in a form more suitable for new minds and new circumstances. For the one thing to be cared for, and to secure being true, is the idea, and not its clothing. It is natural for us to like the clothing we ourselves give to an idea. But by unduly loving our form, we are in danger of being so dazzled by it as to forget the truth which underlies the form, and finally to believe only in the form. Do not be betrayed through vanity, or through the applause of men into that deadly error. Desire, on the contrary, that the idea should have new clothes for every change of circumstances, for every change of the world's thoughts around it. Then, it will do good. But keep the old clothes upon it, and it becomes useless, and is thrown by on the dust-heap of worn out things, until some one comes by, finds it, strips it of the rotten garments, sees that it is a beautiful thing, and re-clothes it! Would you save your thought from that fate? Be like Moses, then, who provided that a different form should be given to his thoughts in Joshua; like Christ, who gave His ideas to twelve men, all different in type, that there might be diversities of gifts, but the same spirit, differences of administration, but the same Lord working all and in all.

So far, then, for the starting of the friendship between Moses and Joshua. How does Joshua first appear before us? It is as the warrior, and he keeps that apparition till near the end of the story. And no figure can well be finer. He is the great soldier, so full of the spirit of war, that it is the first thing he thinks of always, as when descending the mountain he cries, on hearing the shouting and singing, "There is a noise of war in the camp"—the dominant thought claiming all things as its own—; the natural chieftain, whose mighty war-cry always stirred, and may have first given birth to, that peculiar and terror-striking shout with which Israel rushed to battle. We think of Achilles shouting from the trench as we think of Joshua. And the two great battle images we have of him recall the spirit of the Greek hero. We see him by the side of the gorge of Ai, when he had lured the warriors of the city forth, on a rock beside the path, stretching forth his spear towards the city, shouting to the ambush until it rose, and then turning like a lion on the foe he had tricked, surrounded, and now descended to destroy. He is seen again, in the same picturesque isolation, standing on the heights above Bethhoron, spear in hand, against the space of broken light, calling on the sun to halt, and the moon to stay: at his feet the stony valley, filled with the rout of the kings of the Canaanites and the pursuing Israelites, and over them and in the sky, the dark onset of the fierce clouds that poured hail and lightning forth until the people were avenged of their enemies. It is a splendid image of wild war; and he is its centre and its inspiration.

The career, of which that battle was the crown, began almost immediately after the Exodus, more than forty years before, in the fight with Amalek. Moses sent him forth; he returned in triumph, and then began his training. It was an hour of great danger for his future work, for no one can help seeing that his temptation would be to feel that which every Israelite was first taught not to feel—that it was his own arm that had won the fight, and his own genius that had secured it. It is not without reason, then, that the story makes Moses take him up afterwards with him into the sacred mountain, into the awful presence of God's power, and while he went himself into the central darkness, left Joshua upon the outskirts alone, in those dread solitudes. That was enough to take out of a man the sense of his own greatness. What solemn thoughts then were his, what inspiration of his own nothingness, and of God's fulness, what overwhelming awe, we may conjecture, but need not tell. We, who have been alone on the mountains, or on the sea, when a mighty storm was raging, and there was within us also a deep conviction of God, may, perhaps, conceive how deep was the lesson of humility learnt by Joshua during the many days upon the mountain! It was learnt for life, at least. There is not one touch from beginning to end of his course, of any self-exaltation to the exclusion of God. No man could more undividedly carry out the idea that all Israel's victories and success were due to God alone.

But humble as he was made before God, he might have been tempted by his first success to set himself forth as leader instead of Moses. There was cabal enough against Moses had Joshua been inclined to join it; and right glad would the rebels have been of his help. But had he been capable of that, he would not have been capable of governing. The next step in his training was to learn how to obey with love and reverence. Therefore, after he had been solemnized upon the mountain, he became the "servant," the daily attendant of Moses. He lived with him in the tabernacle, doing his work, running to and fro in attendance, learning the duties which should belong to him as leader by being the right hand of the leader; the greatest warrior of the camp in daily obedience to the lawgiver of the camp. And we see why he did this—not because it was useful to him, or gave him a name, but because he needed, out of his strong and simple heart, to express his love and his veneration in delighted service. That is the very best thing which can possibly happen to a man who has in after-life to do similar work to that which Joshua had to do—to manage others and to govern them. It teaches him how to rule; it teaches him the things which must be done, if rule is to be supported; and how to do them, and to get them done. It teaches him that the truest service is that done through love and reverence. It teaches him that the ruler's life must be such as to win love and reverence—that these are the roots of power. It was a lesson thoroughly learnt by Joshua.

Indeed, it seems as if this kind of work on Joshua, this teaching of him to be the obedient, the humble servant, instead of the chief warrior, went still further. It looks as if he were taken away from being the war leader for a time. We do not find him as captain in the wars with Sihon, King of Heshbon, or Og of Bashan. Phinehas and others take the command in these, and Joshua is left with Moses, to all appearance, quietly in the camp. That is curious, but it was wise and good for him—for he was not to be the warrior only. There would fall to his work afterwards the allotment of land to the tribes; the organization of the new settlement; the founding of a government along with the priesthood. To stay with Moses, then, and to learn that which did not belong to his special genius; to drink in something of the law-giver's spirit; to make friends with men like Eleazar, who governed the religious body, and who would be his confidant and adviser—these were things he could not do afterwards, in the midst of the wars of Canaan, and it was all important to learn them now. Therefore, he may have been led to lay aside for a time his special type of work and to do things necessary for the future settlement he had to organize in Canaan.

Again, had he alone led the host he might have thought too little of the ability of others to do his work, or been jealous of any one sharing in it or coming near his glory. He was kept, therefore, in the background for a time, till he learned that there were plenty of men in the host quite fit to lead the children of Israel to victory. It was an excellent lesson. He knew thus the stuff of the men he had to command; he knew whom he could trust; he lost all envy and jealousy of the fame of others; he was ready to give every man under his command his due, to hold himself only as one among many heroes. The little story in the eleventh chapter of Numbers shows how much he needed this. He was angry because two men who had not been appointed by Moses prophesied in the camp. It was the very spirit of the martinet, and, if it had not been checked, would have been the jealous and envious spirit in the commander of an army; and both would have been fatal in Canaan to his influence and success among the hot tempered princes of Israel and the fierce people. As it was, whatever be the reason, Joshua had got rid of all this weak, jealous, and martinet temper when we find him in Canaan. Not one of the complaints, not one of the cabals, such as were made against Moses, were made against him. That which Moses said to him when he carried his jealous tale about the unauthorized prophets—"Enviest thou for my sake, would God all the Lord's people were prophets"—Joshua would have said to any one who reported to him an unauthorized deed of war by one of his companions as dangerous to his supremacy—"Enviest thou for my sake, would God all the Lord's people were chieftains in war." To reach that noble temper was worth his long retreat.

Of course, it holds its lesson for us. It is not to shut ourselves away from all pursuits or objects save those for which we have a special genius; it is to retire sometimes from that we do, or think we do, in a splendid way and in which we get fame, in order to learn the other side of things; to balance and complete our powers; and to do that, not with the self-conscious object of making ourself a greater personality, but because we have met some one like Moses whose qualities we think higher than our own, and whom we admire with all our heart. The giving up for a time of work for which we have a genius, if we have this motive, will do wonders for our character; will check the evils and balance the good of our genius; will enable us to see how well others do that which we think we do so splendidly; and when we get back to our toil will help us to use the powers of others in the best way possible, without their opposition or their jealousy, because we are free from jealousy. It will delight us then to find merit; for we care, not for our own fame in the thing for which we have genius, but for the beauty of the thing itself. Self has been wrought out of us. "Would God," we say, "that all men were musicians, or poets, or great lawgivers." Why? Because it is music and poetry and great thinking that we care for, and their beauty—not for our own fame in these matters. And that, believe me, is the great, the noble, and the beautiful temper. Worldliness, littleness, and conceit cannot breathe in its atmosphere. It is simple and passionate, and modest and heroic. Many English war chiefs have had it, and many men of genius; and in the Bible Joshua is its type.

But though he was thus removed from chieftainship, he knew now his destiny. For now comes the central point of his life in the wilderness on this side of Canaan. He was sent out with eleven others to view the land, and had not the craven spirit of the enslaved Israelites intervened, he would have entered it then as the war leader. For with the sending of him into Palestine was linked his future work as conqueror of the land. Moses drew him apart from the rest and changed his name from Oshea, the Saviour, to Jehoshea, God the Saviour. The new name enshrined his destiny; it dedicated him to his work as captain of the Lord's host, as the winner of the land. It was a kind of baptism; a solemn consecration. Henceforth he knew what he was to do. A mighty, ruling idea was added to his life, and, as events fell out, it guided, inspired, and developed him for many years before he could put it into action. It was a wonderful thing to have this new tenant in his heart, and the change of name was but a faint symbol of the marvellous change the thought must have wrought in his whole character. Imagine the life, the prophecy, the ardour it must have, by its very presence, given to all act and thinking, to every quality of his character. It was like the outbreaking of a springhead of waters in a commonplace land; and it is delightful to picture to oneself the new and passionate thoughts and feelings the warrior must have had as he went along, day after day, with the rest, through the vineyards and fields, and by the villages of the land where his fathers had been, and which he was chosen by God to conquer for his brethren. Those were days one would give years of life to share in and remember.

Full of enthusiasm, he came back, one faithful companion with him taking part in his excitement and courage. And now, at the very height of his eagerness, all his dream was broken and despised. When the people heard the report of the spies, they were terror-stricken, and one of those base outbreaks took place which are prompted by fear. Would to God, they said, we had died in Egypt, or in the wilderness—better to return to Egypt than to fall by the sword of the Anakim. Let us make a captain and get back to Egypt. This was Joshua's first trial, and it was a sharp one. In the bitterness of his disappointment, in the chilling of his hopes, he might easily have been tempted to go with the majority, or to give way to their dread, or to oppose himself to Moses, or to be untrue to the great object of his life—the winning of Canaan. How easy to say—"I will be your captain and take you back to Egypt." How did he come out of it? For in these times when a man is tested, we see the real stuff of which he is made. "And they said"—that is, Caleb and Joshua— "the land which we passed through to search it, is an exceeding good land. If the Lord delight in us, then He will bring us into this land and give it to us, a land which floweth with milk and honey. Only rebel not ye against the Lord." See what vigorous religion, what practical faith in God there is in these men! And now listen to the ring of courage full of faith in their words: "Neither fear ye the people of the land, for they are bread for us; their defence is departed from them, and the Lord is with us; fear them not!" How was this brave cry answered? "All the congregation bade stone them with stones!" It was a sorrowful experience for Joshua. He had quietly to put by his ardour, and his splendid destiny, for many years. But he took two things with him, the two things we find in his speech—great courage, that cheerful courage which is so animating; and great faith in God.

I close by trying to make this story real to our lives. If we are to do anything in life, the time comes sooner or later, when, after much beating to and fro, we find it out and know it. It came to Joshua when Moses re-named him, and gave him his life work. It came to David when Samuel anointed him King over Israel, and he was yet a boy. It came to Christ when he went up to the baptism of John, and was driven into the wilderness to realize the idea of his mission and all its temptations. It came to Wordsworth, and is recorded by him—to take an instance from our own times—on that dewy morning among the hills when he was filled with God, and felt he was a dedicated spirit. It comes to all of us the day we feel—" Here is my work, I will do it and love it, God helping me." It is a solemn time, our name is as it were changed, we are re-baptized, consecrated by God and by our own will.

Some among you may be at that moment now. Then

count the cost, lest having begun you be not able to finish! See what lies before you; search out the land you are going to conquer; go through it step by step, finding out its giants and where they live, its strong places of difficulty and of evil, and all that you have to overcome! And may the courage and faith you have be such, that you may say—"All this is bread for me, the defence of these things is gone. If the Lord delight in me, and I be faithful, I shall accomplish my endeavour."

Some among you may have already begun, or may be well on in the work to which you gave yourself. How have you done it? Well or slothfully? Bravely or fearfully? Having seen the cities of pleasure walled up to heaven, the giants of wrong, the difficulties of the world, have you then come back and cried—"Too hard, would God I had died. Let me get back to Egypt, to my slavish comforts, and my flesh pots!" Then remember this old history. You will not get back to Egypt, you will wander, and it may be die, in the wilderness of a wasted life.

Or is it another thing that has happened. In the very midst of conquest, has some terrible foe stepped in, temptation of pleasure, of evil fame, of self-desire, and led you to give up or to be false to the idea of your work? As you look back, do you know you have been untrue to the ancient inspiration, that it has not been kept pure, that it is trembling on the verge of loss; merciful God, that it is lost, and that you and your work are ruining down the precipice!

It may not be yet. Recall the days when you were baptized into it, when the dew of its inspiration made your soul like a summer garden in the dawn, when ardour filled you and made your life like Paradise, when God's hand was on your shoulder and you heard His very voice—" This is the way, walk ye in it." Or rather recall but little, or only recall enough to gain impulse to go forward. Think of our Joshua, Jesus the great Master. Rise from the dead with him, and follow him into a new life, with faith in the redeeming of wrong by doing right; with faith in God as your Friend—and with the courage of Joshua, begin once more. Be strong and very courageous, and all the Anakim of evil, and even your own evil, will fall down before the faith which labours and the courage that believes.

THE LIFE AND CHARACTER OF JOSHUA.

"Moses My servant is dead; now therefore arise, go over this Jordan, thou, and all this people, unto the land which I do give to them, even to the children of Israel.

"Every place that the sole of your foot shall tread upon, that have I given unto you, as I said unto Moses.

"From the wilderness and this Lebanon even unto the great river, the river Euphrates, all the land of the Hittites, and unto the great sea toward the going down of the sun, shall be your coast.

"There shall not any man be able to stand before thee all the days of thy life: as I was with Moses, so I will be with thee: I will not fail thee, nor forsake thee.

"Be strong and of a good courage: for unto this people shalt thou divide for an inheritance the land, which I sware unto their fathers to give them."—JOSHUA i. 2—6.

THE mourning for Moses was over, and Joshua was left alone; looking his work in the face—a grave and solemn hour. And the thoughts of his soul were the ground of the vision that he saw, when Jehovah spake to him and said—"Moses My servant is dead, therefore arise, go over this Jordan, thou, and all this people, unto the land which I have given them. Be strong and of a good courage. I will not fail thee, nor forsake thee." We see in that the first great thought of Joshua's mind. And the second is, that in the conquered land, and in the conquering of it, the law given by Moses, and its ideas—the unity of God, the overthrow of idolatry, the unity of the people in one

God, the bold moral outlines of the Decalogue, should be rigidly preserved and sternly insisted on. These were the grounds of his life, these the things he went over Jordan to do; and their clearness, and the strength of them, wrought as they were in him by a long education, gave to his life and work their absolute force and lucidity. If you want to do good work, and with overcoming energy, get your thoughts clear, let their outlines be as sharp as those of mountains against the sky.

In this manner, then, the thoughts of the man appear in his vision. In it also appears his character. In another vision said to have been seen by him, the Lord stands at his right hand with a drawn sword. The apparition is such as a warrior would see in dream. To Moses the vision of God comes as the light that no man can approach unto, as the palpable darkness, as the invisible voice that proclaims character—such visions as belong to the prophet and the law-giver—but God comes to Joshua as the Captain of the Host of the Lord. Out of Joshua's character came his vision, and out of our character grows the symbol of our God! As you are, as your nation is, so will be the form of your God, and your nation's God; and as the form is so will the worship be—pure or base, spiritual or idolatrous. Were you to see the vision of your God, how would he appear to you? How should we represent him now? How would the hand of England paint him, were we to collect the vision of the majority? In our peace, would he seem to us as just and pure, as ideal as he seemed to Moses? In our wars, should we see him standing in our front with his sword drawn in his hand, the Captain of our **Host?** Take our national character now, our aims, our lives, our doings with money, with books, with trade, with one another, our objects in politics within and without—and **build** up out of them the image of our God. Should we dare to realize it, **dare to** set it up **in** the exchanges, dare to paint **it on canvas, dare** to proclaim—" Hear, O England, this is the symbol of your God, this the thing you worship!" Is that too difficult to answer? Then build out of your own imagination **the** image of your God, see if you dare to realize that which **is** at the root of the worship of your life. The effort, at **least,** will teach you more than all the preachers can tell you.

The image Moses and Joshua had of God was different for both; but the difference makes no matter if the **symbol be** noble, formed out of a noble thought. For then the love and reverence—the worship in one word—is the same. **It** does not matter in what form we worship, provided that we worship God, and not a devil. It does not matter whether we build up our thought of Him as Conservative or Liberal, Churchman or Dissenter, provided our symbol of Him is noble enough to draw forth the deepest **awe of** conscience, and the deepest love of the spirit. That is **the** point. Moses saw Him as the uncreated Light **and Truth,** Joshua as the Captain of the Host: but both worshipped Him with ennobling love **and awe.**

With these thoughts of God **in his soul,** Joshua went forth to the conquest of Canaan.

How he had won the **country, and of** what kind his character, as warrior now and governor, was in itself, and what it **was** to **others, is** the most convenient division I can make of what I have to say.

1. *In itself.* The first point is the power of Faith in the man; faith in God, faith in the work he had to do, and, therefore, faith in himself. It is faith which gives power in life when the faith is worth the name—that is, when it is belief in realities and not in lies; when it is faith in pure, beautiful and righteous things and persons. If we have such faith, all things are possible, we shall be able to remove mountains. By it, Joshua subdued Canaan; established the nation of Israel; realized that which seemed impossible; and died, having attained his end. It is equally powerful against our spiritual foes, against the evil in us. The man who can truly say—" I believe in God the Father Almighty," is master of the world and of himself. The man who can truly say—" I believe in the forgiveness of sins," is already—not in fact, but in certainty of future righteousness—freed from sin. There is nothing evil in him which will not be finally overthrown.

On such a faith naturally follows the next quality in Joshua's character—the quality of *Courage.* Christ puts the connection between these two things with great clearness— "Why are ye so fearful, oh ye of little faith?" Faith is always the best ground of courage; faith in oneself—the ground of physical courage; faith in the rightness of one's cause, or the rightness of one's thoughts on any subject— the ground of moral courage; faith in God and God's character—the ground of spiritual courage; and when the whole three kinds of faith are wrought together, like three threads of iron in a sword, we have a character like Joshua's, strong and very courageous; mighty in battle, mighty in organization, mighty in making God's ways prevail. And they ought to be wrought together. Physical courage by itself is not a moral quality. It strengthens and gives splendour to moral qualities; but alone, it is to be praised only as good looks, or good health are praised. It needs to be linked to moral acts, or used in behalf of true ideas before it can be highly honoured. Shown in defence of the weak, in sacrifice for love's sake, in death or endurance for others, for the sake of a cause on which vast issues to mankind depend, it shares in the beauty and greatness of these things, and is worthily honoured. The animal quality is made at one with moral, imaginative, and spiritual qualities, and is, in the union, ennobled.

True courage shares, and must share, in the powers of faith, in the passion for right, in the qualities of love. Indeed, of it the same things are true, should we describe it, that are true of love. For courage suffereth long, and is kind; courage envieth not; courage vaunteth not itself, is not puffed up, doth not behave itself unseemly; seeketh not her own; is not easily provoked; thinketh no evil; rejoiceth not in iniquity, but rejoiceth in the truth; beareth all things; believeth all things; hopeth all things; endureth all things.

Out of the clear view of what Joshua had to do, and his faith in its rightness, and in his own power, and out of the great bravery of the man, arose the main quality of his warlike genius, a quality which is all but constant in every great commander; in Alexander, Cæsar, Frederick, Marlborough, Napoleon—*the quality of swiftness.* What is to be done presents itself at once, and, along with that, the action of it, and both are carried out before another man would have made the first step. Twice in Joshua's history we meet this swiftness. The first time was when the five kings of the Canaanites attacked Gibeon; and the second when the northern kings leagued against him, and made their camp at Merom. The sudden rapidity of the march is dwelt on in both cases. Joshua no sooner hears the news than he is afoot. He marches all night, and ere the sleep is out of the eyes of his enemies, his small army is in their midst, shouting its terror-striking war cry.

That is a quality we sorely want in life, and as rarely have; swiftness of decision, swiftness of action. "It belongs to genius," some say, "and it is no use trying for it." No; that is not the true way to put it. It does belong to genius, but it does so because of the steady work, and the long training, and the imaginative exercise of the intelligence which genius has put itself through. These are its roots; these things we all may do—a kind of supernatural insight is not its root. Genius labours, and thinks, and makes experiments, and acts, and tries all methods of action and thought, and never ceases to do this work; therefore, when, after this long energy and practice, a new event or a new crisis calls on it for action— it can think and act swiftly. That is the real source of rapidity, and we may all get a great deal of it in the same way—not all that genius has, but enough to enable us to act more readily than we are accustomed to do. In business, in the conduct of life, in political and literary movements, that is the lesson, and it is just as true in the spiritual life of the soul. Think quickly, act like lightning, would you be great; but remember that quick thought and swift act, without years of work and thought behind them, may bring you—whether you be men of genius or not, and even more if you have genius—to nothing but ruin. Opportunity can only be grasped with success when you have got the hands to hold it first. Therefore Christ said, "Take oil in your vessels with your lamps," else when the cry comes, "Behold the bridegroom cometh," you will have no light, and the door will be shut.

2. And now with regard to Joshua's character in its relation to others. The courage of which I spoke was shown in war, and at that time war was very pitiless. Were we to conduct war as Joshua did, our courage would be stained with crime; but at that time it was not believed to be wrong, but right, to mercilessly slay the enemy. And, indeed, when we make war against a savage nation, I do not think we are one whit better than the Israelites under Joshua were, but as fierce and as bloodthirsty. And Joshua had with his faith the terrible intolerance of the true believer. There is nothing more exterminating than the idea of the one God when it is not modified by the doctrine of the Cross. And Joshua was ruthless, but with the ruthlessness there was also determined thoughtfulness towards his end. He slew, not because he delighted in cruelty, but because he was resolute to get the land for Israel, to fulfil the long desire of Moses, to fulfil what he believed to be the will of God. He slew, not because he loved blood, but because he was fixed in his resolution to overthrow idolatry, and the only way men could think of doing that then was by fire and sword. The world had not seen the more excellent way of Christ. And Joshua won his day. There was no retreat from his

thoughts, no compromise, no pause, no hesitation. When anything stood in the way of completing his thought, he was as stern and pitiless as death. One story represents it all. At the great crisis of the war, at one of those times when in fierce excitement—and Joshua had been living in fire all the day—a man shows what is in him, at the close of the battle of Bethhoron, he took the kings out of the cave, and cast them on the ground, and called to the princes and captains of Israel—" Come near, and put your feet on the necks of these kings." That stamps the man ; that stamped, by one symbolic act, his one great thought of Canaan as the heritage of Israel, into the soul of every man in the host. It was one of those deeds which are never forgotten by a nation as long as the nation lives, which enter into a nation's spirit, and are in it as courage and power.

The same stern, resolute spirit worked towards his own people. When Achan took of the spoil of idolatry, and the first trace appeared of that paltering with the accursed thing which was afterwards to work such woe to Israel, there was no more pity shown than was shown to foes, because Achan's act endangered the ideas Joshua was set to guard and establish. It were well if we were as ruthless with ourselves as he was with Achan; well, if when we are lured away to touch the accursed thing, and to join hands with our idolatries, we should stone till it died the evil in us which stands in the way of our realizing the thoughts which we are bound to fulfil for God and man in our lives. We are not half pitiless enough with ourselves in life. Better than our false and sentimental mercy for evil is the temper of Joshua, the temper of the Puritan ; the temper which says, "Come near, and put your foot on the necks of these kings."

It was thus that Joshua won obedience. He was a man that had to be obeyed, and obeyed he was. To secure obedience is one of the first necessities for a leader of men; nay, for an employer of labour, for the head of a business, for a father in his house, for a master of a school, for all who have to guide. It is the first thing; we must secure it. The only question is, how? To secure it by brutality is finally to lose it. To secure it despotically is to encourage disobedience. To secure it by justice, and by good sense, and by respect for individual liberty, is to secure it as Joshua secured it. Yes; even at this early time, that was his way. Men saw that he kept his word. The carefulness with which he kept it is shown in the watchfulness which in the sack of a city like Jericho could attend to the fate of Rahab. The absolute sanctity of it is shown in the way in which, against his own most cherished thoughts, against the advice of many, he rescued the Gibeonites, who had tricked him and the princes of Israel into a promise of saving them. Though it was to his hurt, though he had been defrauded, his word was sacred. Every soul in the host knew then, that if Joshua claimed obedience, he claimed it on the ground that truth should be respected by him, and justice done.

Nor was his good sense in managing men less. They were a jealous, quick, passionate people with whom he had to do. Had he assumed to himself the airs of a despot, had he ruled them like an Oriental tyrant, he would have won rebellion very shortly. But all through his life he consulted others.

The princes are made assessors with him in all acts; the elders are consulted; the people are told his plans. Eleazar the priest is his bosom friend, and all things are done with his help. Every Israelite felt that if Joshua claimed obedience, he claimed it more because of his being the voice of the best men in the congregation than because he was Joshua.

And it was accompanied by the fullest recognition of personal action. There is a story in which the rough common sense and humour of the man comes out most pleasantly, and which illustrates this (Joshua xvii. 14-18). The tribe of Ephraim, his own tribe, claimed more than their right in the land. They should have no more than their lot, said Joshua; for the rest, they might get what they could by their own hand. "If thou be a great people, get thee up to the wood country and cut down for thyself there, in the land of the giants, if Ephraim be too little for thee." And when they complained and said that the Canaanites were strong, Joshua's rude humour, while he threw them on their own honour and courage, broke out, "Thou art a great people, thou shalt not have one lot only, the mountain shall be thine, and the outgoings shall be thine, for thou shalt drive out the Canaanites. They have iron chariots, and they are strong." Those were pleasant outgoings for a people who wanted to sit still. Even for his friend Caleb, who wanted the rich vintage valley of Hebron, Joshua had the same kind of word. He might have it, but he must win it; and Caleb did win it, driving out the vast sons of Anak. This was the sort of man to make warriors of a nation, and to win their obedience.

And they are all qualities we need if we would be useful fathers, leaders, employers, officers, statesmen; in every position in which by making and winning obedience we have to organize and educate children, labourers, soldiers, a party, a following, or a nation. Is your word sacred, even to your own hurt; can men depend on what you say and feel they can so depend? Are they sure of justice from you, sure that, till you have heard all sides, you will not give sentence; sure that you will put prejudice and party and personal passion aside? Are they sure that even when you are defrauded and cheated, and yet have promised, that you will be careful to be true to the last shred of your promise? Are they certain of your honesty of purpose, do they see that ideas, or your cause, and not your own interest, are first with you? Are they convinced that you do not act hastily, or for your own selfish ends, but with care for the whole community or household or party, by your readiness to listen to or to consult with others? Do they feel that under you they have a chance of self-development; that you look out for their abilities and give them the work they can do well, laying aside your own doing of it and your own glory to promote theirs; and do they find in you, not solitary moroseness, or retiring pride, but a pleasant comradeship, a humour either rough or gay, but full of desire for their honour; a humour that makes them feel that life is not too hard for conquest; which sets hard tasks but laughs as it sets them, in reliance on your courage; and, lastly, do they find in you a clear good sense, which, for the interests of the whole, puts aside all favouritism, which, while you love your own household and your friends, keeps that love for private life, and in public, honours and loves best those who are most useful and most faithful to the interests of the household, the community, or the nation? Then you will be obeyed and merit obedience; otherwise not.

I turn now to Joshua's more secret feelings; to the inner life of the man. We have painted him as he was on the outside, in those matters which belonged to his mission and his relation to his people and his enemies. The poetry in him, the sentiment in him, if he had either, we have not touched.

Of poetry there was not much; his was not the lyric temper. Among a people who sang naturally in verse, his voice was silent, though he made the subjects for songs. But it is not uncommon that such men, at some passionate crisis of their lives, have for a moment found themselves forced to express emotion in a higher form than that of prose. There are many instances of men who have produced a single poem. It was once so with Joshua. He had rushed up all night from Gilgal and fallen on his foes. On the fate of the battle hung the whole fortunes of Israel. All the day he had fought with the enemy, and now they were driving in headlong flight down the steep of Bethhoron. He saw the long, long desire of hundreds of years, the long desire of his master, his own passionate hope fulfilled. Canaan was theirs! It was enough to excite a man who had not slept, who had marched all night, who had fought for a whole day. And now, to heighten his excitement, the storm broke forth, the thunder roared. God spoke in the crash, and the sweeping hail, and the blinding lightning. The wild shout of the people in pursuit reached him on his height, and, in the wild inspiration of the hour, he broke into poetry:—

> "Stand thou still, O sun, upon Gibeon;
> And thou, moon, on the valley of Aialon!"

They may well be his very words. They are some of the oldest words in the Bible, wrought afterwards into the ancient verses of the Book of Heroes, which is quoted in our Book of Joshua. "And the sun was still, and the moon stayed, until the people had avenged them on their enemies." It was no wonder Joshua burst into song, no wonder in the light that followed the storm the simple men of the time saw God's answer to His servant's cry.

That was the first and the last poetry of Joshua. But of the poetry of human feeling, of the sentiment that flows, voiceless, round the love of country, of friends, of home, his life had enough to satisfy imagination.

For forty years he followed and clung to Moses, in daily service. Nothing but love could do that. The strong devotion of the rougher to the finer character, of the practical to the ideal (for it was the ideal part of Moses that won Joshua's love), of which there are many examples in history—that was Joshua's steady romance. Then we may well imagine that there was a close friendship between him and Caleb. Of all the host these two alone remembered Egypt; had seen together, face to face, all the wonders of the wilderness. Of all the ancient host they had alone been faithful to trust and courage. They had together maintained that the Canaanites, huge and powerful as they were, would be as water before their valour. Caleb had the same dash, the same fierce strength, the same indomitable belief in himself, the same spirit of adventure as Joshua. In his old age when he won Hebron, and founded the mighty tribe of Judah in its place, he set into flame his followers for adventure, and the one romantic story of the Book of Joshua, where the women of Judah are shown as the inspirers of chivalric act, is a story of the family of Caleb.

So it is a pleasant thought to think of Joshua and Caleb together in their old age, when both had settled down. What talk they would have had; what memories of Egypt; how the young men must have clustered round them in the evening to hear the tale of the deliverance, of the Red Sea, of Sinai, from the lips of those who alone in the whole of Israel had seen the things; and how closely this strange, isolated relationship must have knit them together! There is no more poetic situation in the whole of the Bible! Consider it, picture that relationship. It carries us out of the tumult of war into the peace of life's eventide, away from the vision of the ruthless conquerors to that of the quiet friends who sat chatting together on the slopes of Gerizim, listening to the music of the many springs that still fall from rock to rock, and hearing in the shouting of the reapers in the valley, so rich in corn that it laughed and sang, the witness and proof of the fulfilment of God's promise to their fathers.

The picture strikes the note of Joshua's old age. When the conquest was over, he sought a home. He found it in the midst of his own tribe, the mighty tribe of Ephraim; in the central valley of Canaan, at Shechem, "the border of the Sanctuary," on which Mount Gerizim looked, "the mountain which the right hand of God had purchased." It was a fitting place to spend the last days of a life which had been lived to secure the promise given to Abraham, Isaac and Jacob. For the country was steeped in the traditions of his fathers. It was on Gerizim's height, the story ran, that Abraham had taken the knife to slay his son, and God had interposed to promise him the land. It was on Gerizim that Melchisedek, men said, had ministered. It was in the valley below that the tribal oak had been consecrated by Abraham. Beneath its shade Joshua spoke, beneath it Isaac had rested and Jacob worshipped. Close by Shechem was Jacob's well, and Jacob's dwelling place for many years. Everything he saw recalled his fathers and the promise, and Joshua's heart swelled with joy as he looked down from his house, and felt that God had done so great a work.

Finally, one great ceremony embodied all his life. There, in full assembly of Israel, he celebrated the fulfilment of the promise by laying the bones of Joseph at last to rest. They had remained, waiting for deliverance, in Egypt, for many, many years. "God shall surely visit you," said Joseph, dying, "and ye shall carry up my bones from thence." They had been taken with them that terrible night, and crossed the sea with the escaping host. They had rested at Sinai, gone through the wilderness, accompanied the conquest—their Palladium, the immortal witness of what Israel had done in Egypt, and was to be in Canaan—and, on this solemn day, of all that Israel had attained. And now, after so many restless years, they were put to sleep at last, in the plot of ground that Jacob had given to his son Joseph. It was the crowning act of Joshua's life.

Yet he lived a long time after that God had given his people rest. It was, to the end, a life of work, quiet but steady — work of arrangement, allotment, consultation, advice. Every week he went to confer with Eleazar. He set up his house, organized the city, build the citadel, secured and wrought together the land he had conquered and the nation he had made. And then, old and stricken in years, beneath the oak of Abraham and Jacob, he called together the people, and made his last farewell, set up the pillar men long remembered, and died, rooting still deeper by his speech in the minds of his nation the two sides of his life ; for he made a covenant with them that they would be true to the invincible God of Moses, and he told them again and again that Canaan, God's promised land, was theirs for ever.

Oh, may we, when our age comes, so live and die ! After long education, after stormy manhood, after unbroken pursuit of our idea, after the wars of life in which we conquer the enemies of our work and place our foot upon their necks—may we sit down in peace, not without friends and love, and build our house of rest, and lay down our thoughts and work, having finished them, as Joshua laid down the bones of Joseph—yet, while we live, be not without work ; supporting and watching the results of all we have accomplished ; by our wisdom dividing and providing new toil for others ; making our experience useful ; happy with our old companions ; delighted with the young warriors of life whom we encourage ; and bidding, finally, farewell to all, before we go to God, with solemn words of warning, hope and love—none better than those of Joshua to his people—"Cleave to the Lord your God;" "Be very courageous to keep the law of God;" "One man of you shall chase a thousand"—hear the old warrior ring—"Take good heed that ye love the Lord your God;"—and at last with our last breath, rejoicing in the fulfilment of the work of life in God, have utter joy in death as we look back on the duties we have done, and the long years we have fulfilled.

"And behold this day I am going the way of all the earth, and ye know in all your hearts and in all your souls, that not one thing hath failed of all the good things which the Lord your God spake concerning you; all hath come to pass unto you, and not one thing hath failed thereof."

To the last, triumphant faith—a warrior's courage!

[July 1, 1883.]

THE LATER CHOICE OF LIFE.

"And it came to pass, when they had brought them forth abroad, that he said, Escape for thy life; look not behind thee, neither stay thou in all the plain; escape to the mountain, lest thou be consumed!"
GENESIS xix. 17.

THERE is no need for me to explain or to rationalize this story, to show how far it may be historical and how far not. All that is waste of time. Only one thing is historical in it, and that is the destruction of the cities of the plain of Siddim by a volcanic earthquake, with its usual accompaniments. With regard to the rest of the tale, it is better at once to class it under the title of a legend, invented by the writer, with a patriotic and a religious purpose, out of some scanty materials. We are then enabled, taking it as such, to get out of it such lessons for life as we derive from other religious legends invented by men who, filled with the experience of human life, and eager to warn and teach, embodied their thoughts in a story. Take, then, the characters as real in the realm of poetry, but not historical; take the events as we take the events in the legend of Achilles or Arthur, and let us see what the early artist meant and how far his poetic representation of a scene in the drama of human life can speak to us across the centuries. As in all fine artistic work, the characters are made so real that we may treat them for our purpose as if they had been true. Lot and Abraham stand out as representative of two types—of types now among us, and the events which exercise them are such as, in their spirit, may happen now.

Some time before, matters had come to a point in the life of Lot and Abraham. Their servants quarrelled, and it was necessary, for the sake of peace and friendship, that they should break up their united lives and dwell apart; and Abraham, in his grand and easy way, said to Lot, "Take your choice, and what you leave I will have for mine." And Lot chose the rich valley, and Abraham took the mountain and the pilgrim life; not that he would have chosen any other, but the writer of the story made it so. So Abraham was left alone with God and high thoughts and plain living, to live apart, till death, his life of faith; and Lot went down to the cities where ease and wealth and comfort were, among men who in sin and sloth had forgotten judgment. And if he were vexed, as a later writer said, by the foul life around him, he seems to have borne it with enough complacency. At any rate, while Abraham's character deepened into grandeur, Lot's degraded into weakness.

Character, then, hangs on a choice of this kind, and it is a choice which does not belong to youth, but to later life. Both these periods of life have their hour of decision, but it is the later one of which we think to-day.

The fable is always true which represents the choice which has to be made at the entrance into life. Two women stand before us, clad each in the vesture of their character. One, with a majestic beauty, half of which is strength, and on whose face is the loveliness of experience and power, will guide us to the mountain paths where every step is labour, and the end of which is wisdom and force, and power to give power and blessing. The other, on whose face is the beauty of the wind and the flowers, and whose eyes dance with the brightness of pleasure, and whose feet, with the lightness of impulse, will guide us to the stream-fed valley, where every wish breaks into flowers at our feet and the sunlight is warm as love. And the end of it is slavery, and weakness, and weariness, and the knowledge of wrong that cannot be set right. And as we look back, the valley of past years is waste, and the flowers dead, and the stream dry.

Then, from the end of the valley, where the mountain is pathless, we must, if we would escape, ascend, for the abyss is before us. But with what torment is the mountain climbed then! It is well for us if there is left enough of fierce impatience in our hearts to carry us over rocks and brake, before the night fall, to the way of strength and renunciation!

So is it in youth. But even if we have taken the mountain path at the beginning, or even if we have escaped from the valley of pleasure, and are now pursuing the upward climb, and have won our way half way up the mountain side of life, is there no further choice? Do the two fair women never appear again? Yes, in later life. There is then an hour of decision on which hangs the weightiest issue possible! A sudden turn that seems fortuitous, comes in the path; some event has made it, in our own life or in another's—such as this quarrel between the herdsmen of Abraham and Lot; or a new element enters from without into our lives, and, all in a moment, we meet the two women again, face to face! But their form is changed, and their offers are changed, and we are changed. We have now won wisdom and knowledge, great or little; the tools of life are in our hands and we know how to use them; we have gained power, and that conscious sense of it which doubles its capacity. We have won, not only power, but also the knowledge of our weakness, of what we cannot do, so that we can avoid waste of energy. We are equipped, and our step is easy up the mountain, if our heart is light. What do the women want? Why do they stop the way? Well, the time has come when we must choose between the world and God; between a life of slavery and a life of simplicity. And she who of old was Pleasure stands before us now—superb, with wealth in her hand, and a crown ablaze with gems of fame upon her head, and with the pride of life glittering in her eye—the Queen of the World, who will give us many things, almost all things but Peace, and Love, and God. In her skirts are hidden cares, and cravings, and insatiableness, and coldness of heart; and round her feet serpents are crawling—Meanness, the Deceitfulness of wealth, and Lying, and Dishonesty, and Vulgarity of heart. "Come with me," she cries, "turn the stones of this desert into gold! There is a valley close by here, in the heart of the hill, where you shall have worship, and pleasure, and ease, and luxury. Climb the arduous hill no more; you have done enough of aspiration! The summit of the Ideal is cold and lonely; cling to the glory of wealth and ease and to your own will—to the material and the practical. Thousand thousand are my followers, and the whole valley is warmed with fires—not with this sunshine of the mountain side, broken by storms, so that you have no peace as you climb! You shall have all things you need for outward life." And the promises dazzle our eyes and heart, and we yield to her voice, and the rest of life is given to that service—a service that changes into slavery. "And Lot lifted up his eyes, and beheld all the plain of Jordan that it was well watered everywhere, as the garden of the Lord; and he chose it, and pitched his tent towards Sodom," and came to dwell therein.

But it may be we pause awhile, taught, perhaps, by the pain we have suffered in escaping from the valley of Pleasure, and listen to the other woman. She has no splendid robes, no glittering crown, no horn of plenty in her hand, nor is there on her face that audacious beauty. Her garment is of silver-grey, woven without seam from the top to the bottom, and in its folds lurk no hidden things, for fold it has none. And her head is hooded, but the hood does not hide her lovely face where many sorrows have been, but where peace is conquering sorrow; nor her eyes, in whose depths is seen, far off, perfect joy; nor her smile, downcast, but noble, which has the promise of infinity; and in her hand is the secret of love. "Come," she cries, "with me, and climb the mountain still. We shall have storm and pain, but natural shall be the sunlight, and the pleasures shall be noble. And the mountain top of the Ideal is not so cold and not so lonely, for God is there and the assembly of those who never ceased to strive; lovers of righteousness, lovers of beauty, lovers of truth; those uncontented save with perfection. You shall not have wealth, but you shall keep wonder; you shall not have the praise of men, but you shall retain admiration, hope, and love; you shall not have the wisdom of the world which is involved, but you shall retain the wisdom of the child among the powers of faithful work; and yours shall be the simplicity of humility, and singleness of aim, and fidelity to truth, and carelessness of debasing cares. No sensuous pleasure is in my power, nor splendid display, but you shall have the unpurchased joy which receives all the joy of the universe into its breast because it thinks not of itself; and the splendour of God shall be your delight. I will give you no outward things, but I will make you noble within; and when you are dead, in the seed that you have sown shall all families of the earth be blessed."

A wonderful voice it is, and great is the beauty of the woman; and as we climb with her, more and more lovely shine her eyes, and deeper is the light within her countenance. Follow her, for in her hand are the issues of true life, since in her hand is Love. Follow her, if you have the heart to do it; but if you follow, look not back with regret, lest you lose her perfect joy, nor think for one instant of all the glittering things which fall on the path of that stately and rich Dame whose hand you have put aside for ever. Choose, and cling to your choice. Love not the world, nor the things of the world. And Abraham went forth a pilgrim, and dwelt in the uncitied plains and in the hills, and spoke with God, and wandering, built at every place he dwelt in an altar to the Lord; a stern and simple life, but blessed within with righteousness.

That is the choice of later life, and then, more even than in earlier life, are the words true—"Strait is the gate and narrow the way that leadeth unto life, and few there be that find it." For a hundred that go with Abraham, there are thousands that go with Lot. And what do they get in the end thereof? When the latter days came, what has become of Lot, and what of Abraham? what of him that went with the World, and of him that went with the Ideal?

Let us follow the story, for though it could not paint all the types of those who take to the life of comfort, and getting on, and self-pleasing, and inward death, yet it paints one type in Lot, and sketches another in his wife. They lived in peace for years, when, all in an instant, their easy life broke up in judgment and dismay; such dismay and judgment as falls on many now in loss of fortune, loss of honour, loss of health, in the fires and earthquake of life— things which, when they come upon a heart like Abraham's, simple, and pure, and strong, and full of faith in God, awaken in it vigour and joy of battle, and certainty of conquest; but which, sweeping in on a heart softened and enervated like Lot's, are ruin. Clanging in his ears, so long lulled to the music of luxury, came the cry, "Escape for thy life, escape to the mountains, lest thou be consumed!" He had enough of faith to obey the call, but with what miserable weakness it was obeyed! All his character had been enfeebled. He had had strength enough not to join in the wickedness around him in the city, but not strength enough to leave it; content to live among evil, yet soothing his soul with the thought that he was free from it; lingering on in habits of life which were stealing away, day by day, his moral and spiritual power; doing all his goodness by halves; slipping further and further away from righteousness: enervated, softened, unmanly; incapable of grasping any crisis firmly; incapable of seeing absolute necessities; clinging to situations that had become impossible; shutting his eyes to the hour of judgment, like us, when for years we have abandoned the mountain life. He had to be forced away—so vivid is the story. He dreaded the night journey, begged with unmanly wailing for a respite—few words in the Bible are more abject than his prayer for Zoar; all his life long "letting I dare not wait upon I would." This was the character wrought by the world in his heart. So he fled away, helpless, unsupported, inwardly complaining, into the night, while behind him the fire fell upon his home. But he took with him into solitude the character he had made for himself. When morning came he looked back over a wasted life, and looked forward to a lonely end—his memory haunted with sights of sin, his soul sick with its own weakness, dogged to the grave with the sense of miserable failure. Follow him to the end, and see how the lesson deepens. He feared to remain in Zoar, the terrors were about him. He fled to the mountain to live in fruitless solitude. Then drunkenness, the sin of the lonely, stole over him, and in his family was the trail of abominable evil—and then there is no more. He goes out in silence—and it is best.

Is this a legend of three thousand years ago? Why, it happened yesterday, down in the City—here, in the West End! How do I know it is not happening at this instant, while I preach, in the hearts of some among us? For if it be not outward ruin through inward weakness that we see, it may be the inward ruin which we cannot see with our eyes. The man who will not separate himself from the evil of the world because he enjoys the life which accompanies that evil, who overlooks wrong lest he should be disturbed in his comfort, who shelves the convictions of his soul that he may not offend those whom yet he thinks untrue, who suffers the sensual while he claims to be righteous, who sits in the gate of Sodom, and yet tries to enter the gate of Heaven, who would turn the crown of thorns into a crown of flowers, and the cross into a bed of roses, may be delivered from this vile life when judgment falls, but it will be so as by fire—a brand plucked from the burning, as the prophet called Lot; but even delivered, he is miserable; a weak, broken, self-despised, guilt-beset, complaining, empty man. Nothing is left within but the desert, and silence and death are his only friends.

While you can, before it be too late, ere the judgment fall, before the hand of the driving angel is on your shoulder, escape to the mountains, seize, at whatever cost, the life of Abraham. Better to die in that effort than to live any more in the world of weakness and pleasure, in the slumber of sloth, or the greed of wealth.

Lot had some character, and it was spoiled; but there was another with him—his wife—who seems to symbolize those persons whom the mere life of wealthy commonplace and comfort forbids to grow. They may have a character, but it is never developed. I might sketch her from fancy as the type of many: nothing actually evil, nothing actually good, insensibly taking the hue of the society and times in which she lived: not sufficiently astir to swim herself with the stream of impulse, but unresistingly borne with it; in one point alone her attachments strong, in a blind, cat-like, clinging to the habits of the life and place she was accustomed to, until all new action and new thought seemed intolerable.

So, she made ready to go with her husband, but drawn aside by long established ties, still loitered in the well-known streets—torpid with long comfort, loath to let go the old, loath to begin the new; now wishing to gather and take with her the things with which her life was bound up; now wishing again to see her friends; wholly confused with the sudden summons to depart and without a grain of faith in its necessity, for she had no world beyond her senses—lingering, lingering on in passive sensuousness, till it was too late. Flying alone across the plain, encumbered with the relics of her old life, like many a one whose story is told in the overthrow of the cities of Campania, she was overtaken by the deadly vapour, fixed in death, and round her piled the storm-driven salt, a monument of the doom that attends delay when Heaven and earth are come together in judgment.

It is a vivid story, and all the more vivid to us when we take it with a symbolic meaning, as Christ himself took it. "Remember Lot's wife." When the day of proof and choice arrives, when life comes to a crisis, and God speaks at last, it is not the time for loitering, for clinging to the past, for trying to carry with you into the future the relics of the old. Escape for thy life, cries God, escape to the mountain world; the very angel's hand is felt upon the shoulder, pushing us forth—and yet we linger enthralled putting off the new duty; loving the ancient house of life, passively clinging to the habits or sins of life, unable to move till it is too late—and the judgment comes. For life we are fixed into the death from which we might have broken away. The vapours of habitual wrong stifle the soul, and our life is salt—dull bitterness, or, if we waken into anger—as some of this type have done at last—savage self-contempt.

So, in these two examples worked the world. The fate of neither could have come in youth or early manhood. It belonged, in both cases, to later life. It was the result of a choice made in the midst of life. As I have said before, so I say again, it is not so much in youth, as when we have all our powers clear and our character formed, that the real crisis comes. Each has his own testing, but in our society the most common is that of which I have spoken. Will you turn then to the life of the world, or will you live the simpler life that Abraham lived? Which character shall be yours, for that is the best way to put it, and what shall be your end?

We have dwelt on Lot, and on the miserable fate he made; on his wife and her piteous close. It is like passing out of heavy vapour into the freshness of the hill tops, to pass away from Lot to think of Abraham. From the hour he left his ancient country, he had never wavered. His life had the blessedness of the continuity of goodness. Day by day he went onward towards the ideal. He looked for a city that had foundations, whose builder and maker was God. Day by day he endured hardness, and his soul was made strong. Day by day he grew in power and in gentleness. God, and not the sickly life of the cities, dwelt within him. Mighty ideas were his, and matchless joys; and the stars of Heaven were more vocal to him in age than in youth. Life was simple; yet, it had the changes in it of noble love, of a heart into which flowed, because it was empty of self, all the wonder of the universe.

It is not an old story that I tell you; it is a story of to-day. The life of Abraham is a life you may yourselves lead, it is a character you may yourselves possess. But to lead the life, and have the character, you *must* give up the world.

[February 4, 1883.]

FALSE FERVOUR OF HEART.

"Fervent in spirit; serving the Lord."—ROMANS xii. 11.

In a society so full of opportunities for excitement as ours is in this great city, and where the culture of the feelings has gone so far and wandered over so many strange paths; where men and women have wearied out so much of life that they are either quiet from lassitude of experience, or excited to find new experiences which will kindle fresh desires and fresh pleasure, it is hard to draw the line between noble and ignoble excitement—between noble and ignoble quietness; and every day sees persons who impel themselves, or permit themselves, into extravagant and erring excitements—who, curious of new sensations, seek them unwearily; others who, wearied with sensations they have had, or afraid to have sensational life of any kind—vaguely fearing that which they have not experienced—either sink slowly into monotony as a kind of repose, or deliberately choose it as their portion because it is safe.

It may not be without use to analyze a portion of the life of such fervent characters and to see what can be wisely said about it.

There are those, then, who cannot bear a quiet life, or, rather, a life which is not always moving, either without or within. They do not dislike a life which seems quiet, provided it has its emotions minute by minute. They do not always want great emotions, but they do want them numberless and varied if they are not great. And their habit is not only to seek them eagerly if they have not got them, and to be restless, impatient, indignant without them, but also, when the emotions come or are discovered, to fling themselves wholly into them; to set sail the moment the wind begins to blow, and to clap their hands with joy as they round the pier head, and, leaving the dull harbour behind, feel the waves dancing under their vessel, and an unknown sea before them. "This time," they think, "they may find the happy isles, and, at least, there is life in the sea and wind and in the battle with the storm." What may happen is nothing to them! Even if they know there is danger in the new emotion they will not forecast the danger, or, if they do, it has its own charm. Curiosity is so awake that it seems as if it would never sleep again, and the Unknown lures them forward with irresistible witchery. "If I die," they say, "I die; but, at least, I shall have had my day! If others are injured in my impulse, let them look out for that! I am not their keeper; and if they are happy before they die, or before they have sorrow, neither sorrow nor death will matter much to them!"

But mostly they do not argue or think thus—they act without thinking. The movement, the thrill, the pleasure of each moment are enough for them. Away, far away, they sail—fervent in spirit, indeed—but not serving the Lord!

Sometimes they are fortunate, when the impulse happens —for it is all chance—to be a good one, and to move within the sphere of natural morality; but just as often—and far more often, indeed—they are shattered or wrecked, or they wreck and shatter others. The impulse towards the unknown, or the emotion they encourage, either happens to be wrong or holds wrong in its end. If it be wrong, they find themselves, when too late, in the midst of the wrong and fond of the wrong. Then, even though they see the rocks, they rush upon them rather than retreat. It may be, they think, they will get through the breakers and land upon the blissful isle!

Or the impulse, in itself right and noble at first, is changed into wrong because they think only of their own pleasure in it, and not of the nobleness of it. And they have the horror at the end of finding they have spoilt in themselves or in others that which was the glory and perfection of life, turned the fine gold into clay, changed the swift summer wind into a tempest, made desolate the garden by forcing all its flowers into hurried bloom! That is a dreadful disenchantment; and, after it, life for a time is shattered. They creep back to the harbour like a disabled ship.

Such characters and such things are common enough, though they are secret; and half of the complaints of life, half the idleness of society, half the want of faith in God, half the irreligion of the day is caused by these uncurbed impulses; by emotion yielded to for its charm, and selfish because it is thoughtless. And these persons are dangerous to themselves and dangerous to others, because the swift feeling and keen life they possess and give are, in the midst of a dull society, the most attractive thing in the world. I am inclined to say that this reckless fashion of living, of yielding in a moment to the moment, is more wicked and does more harm, than guilt which all the world recognizes as guilt. The real root of it is selfishness of a kind which seems to make great sacrifices; and there is nothing so dangerous as selfishness which wears the garb of high emotion; which, seeing the forbidden fruit, mistakes the thrill of curiosity and the rush of feeling for noble enthusiasm and lofty love, and takes it, imagining, "This is good for food and pleasant to the eyes, and to be desired to make one wise, and because *I* like it, it will be good for others, and pleasant to them, and will make them wise." Thus, these fervent characters seem to care for and to think of others, but yet it is only their own joy, their own satisfaction, their own winning of their goal for which they care and of which they think. The more selfish they are, the more they strive to convince themselves that they are unselfish. It is the sole homage that they pay to virtue!

Of course, they are not calculating or cold. I do not speak of those who seek excitement and who do not run its risks, who take its pleasures but keep their own life safe—not of those, almost the vilest of mankind—but of those who take all the risks; who do not think until they reach their goal, or until they are wrecked, of their own security or their own danger, and who are so far unselfish. These please themselves in thinking of how unselfish they have been—for it is natural to dwell on and see what is good; but truly the goodness is a small matter. It is rather not goodness at all, but only the negation of the worst evil.

Well, after the wild sail and the storm are over, they return all but wrecked, exhausted, shattered, to the harbour; often leaving behind them their companions drowned in the sea. What happens then? Many things, and many are the phases they go through, according to character and circumstances.

First, there are those who only wait to refit the ship to begin again; and the moment they are rested, and have gone through their remorse—which only lasts as long as they are tired, and is, in fact, neither spiritual nor moral; that is, it has no leaning even towards repentance, but is only physical—look out for a new excitement, whistle for a new wind, and set forth on a new voyage to face a new storm with all their ancient recklessness. In fact, after a month or two of quiet, life is intolerable until it is again seeking some new excitement, devouring some new path to some untried shore; and, once more they are not only as reckless for themselves as in the past, but as reckless for others whom they carry with them.

And so they lead their lives, often to the very close, until they are either broken to pieces on the high seas and sink in the night, or until decay and old age beset them; and they pass on to the grave, tormented by the memories of pleasures they cannot fulfil, or sitting alone by the fireside of the heart where all their life lies burnt to a heap of dead ash, and opposite them, eye to eye, and always silent, their Fetch, their second self, watching them with intolerable scorn, and often rising to embrace them, and smite itself into them, till they know not which they are, themselves or their self-scorn. That is a pleasant close of life!

(2.) There is another phase of return. It is when, having come back to harbour, they eagerly desire to sail away again, but are unable: either opportunity fails, or circumstances tie them down, or they are restrained by society. Then they acquiesce sulkily in the fate which fetters them, and live a life which they hate and which they think a slavery, though the lash of it is in their own hands, and laid on by themselves. They are quiet enough to the outward eye, rarely flashing forth, but within, the ceaseless strain abides, the ceaseless anger against monotony, the ceaseless hatred of the still waters of the haven, the ceaseless yearning for the waves and the wind, and the watch upon the prow for the undiscovered isles of joy. They will not turn to find life and interest in the present, to work, or to delight in the peaceful, simple, common things around their anchored ship. All their passion is in the past, except that which in the present desires, in thoughts by day, in dreams by night, to repeat the past in another voyage. Two things consume that life—the secret, lonely, down-pressed longing, and that which is the longing's child—the devouring weariness of unexcited life. There are hundreds who live and die in that condition, and the only good to be said of it is negative—"It is not apathy."

(3.) There is another phase. It is when the voyage and the storm being over, the ship has stolen sheltered into harbour, and the owner casts anchor with a sigh, and never wishes again to tempt the deep. These are they who do not go forth again, not because they repent of wrong, but because they have no desire left, and no courage. They fear the wind and the waves, or they are drained dry. "Ask me no more," they say: "give me the still repose; even sleep, if I may rest from tossing; even monotony—day after day the same, no trouble; minute sliding into minute, hour into hour, the same soft quiet things always; and if stagnation come—well, I can endure it better than the tempest."

That is very easy to ask for, but it is not so easy to attain. For the natures which ask for it are not capable of monotony; and if the day be given to self-quiet, to slumbrous ease; if it be not filled with duties which take them out of themselves, and waken and kindle love and work for others—they begin to brood. The memories of past delight, past excitement, past hours when they rode upon the crest of the wave come thronging back, without their pain, without their dismay, without their danger—and, therefore, without a certain redeeming quality—and weave their enchantment round them: and they live in them, unable to work because of their thraldom; restless as a wild beast in his den; wholly enslaved by them—yet all the time knowing that they dare not seek them again; that they would not, if they had the chance; that they have no energy left to set sail and bear away over the deep—enchanting themselves with impalpable dreams, and despising themselves because the dreams are impalpable; and sunk in self contempt deeper and deeper still, because they fear to realize their visions, and yet are enslaved to the imagining of them. They have all the evil of their imaginations, and none of their good; all the death and corruption of them, and none of the movement and life of their reality; all the unhinging thought without the kindling effort; all the hunger and thirst and craving, without one grain of food, one drop of water—soaking day by day into themselves, consumed like a rag in an acid; eaten away by inward scorn; made vile by fear, and useless by sloth, until they rot to death at anchor in a stagnant sea. It is a dreadful fate; and though it is always silent, and therefore unknown, it is the most common of those of which I speak.

These are the phases—and they belong to those who are fervent in spirit, or have been in the beginning—but who are not serving the Lord. They are serving self, pleasure, excitement, sloth, their own will. And if they would escape, they need to make a mighty effort, and to call on God to be their helper. It will not do for them, with this fervent temper, to fight with these desires face to face, as we fight with enemies, for the fighting with them is thinking of them, keeping with them; and even when we beat them down, their face is too fair for us to lift the sword to slay them. On the contrary, we lift them from the ground in pity and in love. They are dearer than before, and we are enslaved again. There is but one way; it is to replace them by other and nobler passions, which, while they kindle equally, and need as keen a pursuit, do not exhaust themselves or exhaust us, but grow more kindling as they are better known, and bring with them a fire which does not burn away. The excitements of earth lash us from without into speed, and while our power lasts, the speed is joy; but the joy passes with the power, and leaves us weak and cold. The excitements of Heaven rise within us in a well of life, and the more they rise, the more desire they have to spring upwards. The joy they bring is sweeter and fresher the more we drink of it. They have the powers of their own life, and they keep us strong and warm of heart. It is only these divine passions that drive out earthly passions which are wrong, or wrong-bringing; and they drive them out by replacing them. The soul is not left empty, swept, and garnished; it is filled and contented.

Would you conquer, you must win a conscious love of God, passionate desire to be His child in goodness and love, in purity and truth. There is no hope of rest until you know nothing in heaven or earth so dear as to see His smile of approval and to hear His voice in your hearts, until you work out your love of God in love of man, and have as much passion in giving up your self as you had before in satisfying it. There is no chance of salvation from the tyranny of your self-will until you set body, soul, and spirit, pulling together mightily, into your work, with the old eagerness, the old pursuit, the old impossibility of sloth, the old delight in looking forward, hour by hour, to see the undiscovered land. Give the effort all your powers; invent new means, discover new plans, realize new hopes by putting them into form, conceive new faiths for man, and act up to your faith, and work on men for God your Father, who, with you, desires their life; and for Christ your Master, who, with you, dies that man may live. Then you will escape. But it is no easy matter. Indeed, it needs a desperate effort; and were it not that we are not left to ourselves to make it, but that there is One that works with us in love, and causes us to feel His love, and who secures to us the strength which, by an unchanging law, is the fruit of every effort towards right which is made with truthfulness, we might well despair, so silently fierce, and so long protracted is the struggle out of passionate self-will into the sacrifice of self to righteousness, and into joy in the sacrifice. Every atom of force in us will have to be given to the winning of love of things which have nothing to do with that which we loved of old, but which demand *its* surrender as the first condition of their love. It is that surrender which is inevitable, and it is that which, for a time, makes the effort almost unendurable. There must be no relaxation of watchfulness; daily, hourly, minute by minute, the soul must stand to its arms. All things which soften or relax the heart must be put away; even innocent and beautiful things, until they come with the new life and not with the old within them; all past associations, until there is no fatal tenderness about them. We must die, and be buried, that we may rise again.

Above all, we must not despair if at first we fail again and again. Courage and hope are ours in God, and despair is the meanest and vilest vice of man. Soon, if we pray and work we shall gain contempt of pain, and before long the struggle will begin to please. The old joy of the waves and winds will rise, and the old excitement kindle and rejoice the heart; but that excitement is now concerned with conquering sin, and claiming and finding righteousness—and it endures. There is no exhaustion, but hourly increasing power; and, as before, with the same rapture, but with how different a goal, we stand upon the prow of the ship of life, eagerly looking forward to the happy days, now almost at hand, when we shall have won freedom from evil, pure light, rejoicing love, union with mankind, communion undisturbed with God; at last, at last, a life impassioned for things which neither exhaust nor wreck the heart, nor in themselves decay. "Fervent in spirit, yet serving the Lord."

[February 11, 1883.]

THE FERVOUR THAT SEEKS MONOTONY.

"Fervent in spirit; serving the Lord."—ROMANS xii. 11.

THERE are those in this stirring world who are by nature quiet, and who prefer the quiet life. They do not know the impulses which beset those who are fervent in spirit, nor what it is to feel that in the space, as it were, of a moment, they are swept out of the harbour into the wild sea, and feel the gale blowing in their heart. Their life, when it moves, only rocks at its anchorage. Day after day, hour after hour, it is much the same; the same duties are done in the same way, the same hours kept, the same thoughts considered and feelings felt, from morn to night. They know, when they wake, all they will do and probably think of throughout the day; and it is only when some shock of fortune, or illness, or bereavement comes, that the calm of their life is broken. And the quiet suits them, and they suit the quiet. Such a life may be a happy one, and is often very happy; but it has one possible evil, or, shall I say, one temptation. It may become lazy; and the fruit of laziness is monotony; and monotony, endurable in youth, becomes a source of disease in later years and in old age. And the moment it is felt as disease, the quiet comfort of the life is over. It gnaws at our heart, and we become uneasy, nervous, troubled, not knowing what to make of ourselves, or what to do with ourselves. We are like a living ship which should feel the dry rot in its timbers, and dreads the day when it will sink, all standing, at its anchorage. There are two ends which may come upon us then; one is the increase of self-dread, self-irritation, until life is unbearable; and the other is the passing through the irritation to the other side of it, into a dead apathy; and I know not which is the worse.

There is no need of such an end; it can be kept at bay. The quiet life may remain usefully, happily, gently quiet to the end; and the heart live, sufficiently stirred not to become stagnant, and having the beauty of quietude—the sunset lights, rosy and of peaceful pearl, around the harboured ship, when all the world and we are old. But to gain this sweet peace and gentle joy, we must prepare our hearts, if we are of this quiet temper, towards this end. It will not come of itself; and what we must do is the same—with modifications which our own character will naturally make —as those who are fervent in spirit, but who choose the quiet life, will have to do. Both these—the quiet and the ardent who want to be quiet—need a similar preparation for the end of life. What that preparation is, and its method, will be the subject of my next sermon. Meanwhile, I must describe those ardent hearts who outwardly resemble those that are quiet, who even seem monotonous because they resolutely repress their fervour, who either determine to choose the quiet life, or are forced into it by circumstances.

These can never be really monotonous. I do not say that they are not often forced into an outer life of monotony. Of course they are; and there are few trials deeper in the world than those the fervent spirit endures from the fetters of a prisoned life. But prison it in circumstances as you please, it is not monotonous within! Nay, often the storm is all the wilder within, because it cannot get forth and spend itself in expression.

I have spoken of those who burst through their barriers, or who, having no barriers, let themselves loose, and, in reckless self-abandonment, or in useless hopelessness and barren longing after self-abandonment, lost the fruits and good of life—of the fervent in spirit who would not serve the Lord!

To-day I speak of those who, though ardent in heart, are not reckless, who neither wreck themselves nor others, and who, in this self-repression, run into other dangers—danger of idleness, danger of apathy, danger of loss of the ideal, danger of evil sadness.

1. There are those—fervent in spirit—on whom a life of monotony is not enforced, but who seek it because it is safe. Their motive is to guard themselves. They select circumstances which bring no disturbance with them; they make modes of daily action which have no excitement; they put aside books, art, poetry, music—anything that stirs and thrills the nerves or the sleeping love of excitement in them. They shut all the windows of the heart and let their intellect act alone.

It is very well, and sometimes it succeeds if the will be strong, and if these persons can always guard against the rush of circumstance. But the motive is not the right one nor is the self-treatment they pursue prudent or right. The motive, being for self-safety only, keeps them locked up with themselves, whereas their only true safety is in being fervent in love of others, so as to lose self-thought altogether. The self-treatment they pursue only battens down the fervent spirit under hatches; and, in the imprisonment, ardour of heart loses self-command and changes slowly its good into evil. It needs the open air, needs to be drilled and exercised into obedience to righteous will, and in free movement; needs not to be crushed, but to be directed rightly; not to be left untrained, but to be educated; not to be imprisoned and beaten down, but to be exalted by noble motives and filled with righteous eagerness. Otherwise, it remains as wild as if no trouble had been taken with it, and is more wild than it was when its possessor was young — nay, often it is maddened by imprisonment. And then, if a crisis should come, if circumstance should dash open the doors of the heart and let the prisoner free, there has been no safety secured. The ardent nature issues forth, reckless from confinement, and, since it has had no education, and gained no principles of love of others, and is furnished with no lofty and impassionating motives of the nobler kind, it avenges itself, seizes on the whole man or woman, and the ruin and the shipwreck are worse even than of those who had never been cautious, never sought for safety. And thereof come, in the end, burning remorse, hatred of the wrong-doing, and hatred even deeper of the old life of peace. The whole of life is as if a fire had passed over it!

2. There are others of these ardent spirits who choose to make their life monotonous in another fashion. They make no effort, they are satisfied to do nothing, and think of nothing. They determine to love nothing, to give them-

selves away to nothing. "Let me keep my soul unoccupied," they say, "my heart empty; so shall I be freed from the great peril of thinking of myself, of wondering how I shall be more happy, of caring for anything, of indulging in any curiosity. I will lay the oars in the boat, shut my eyes, and drift with the stream, and my sleep shall be without dreams. As to the day, let trifles fill it, the froth of life—nothing which can stay me a moment, nothing which I need do more than touch, and while I touch despise."

There are soulless persons who can so live always; without a heart, without a brain, dim zoophytes of men and women; but they are not these of whom we speak. These have the ardent heart; have will, if they choose to realize it; have a soul, if they would not starve it; might fill their life brimful with emotions, thoughts, and actions, if they would, and make it populous with humanity. But they choose the other line of conduct—choose to have their house of life empty, swept and garnished. What is their fate? It is wholly impossible that they should go on in this way for long. They cannot bear emptiness, and if they will not fill their heart with divine and noble love, with sweet and glorious effort, with the laughter and joy, the sorrow and pity of humanity, with all the angel-graces which excite without exhausting—why, we have the wisdom of Christ to tell us what will happen. Seven devils come and dwell in this house of life, and the last state of that man is worse than the first. It is at your greatest peril, if you are fervent in spirit, that you leave your heart empty, your soul unimpelled, your life without work, your brain unpeopled. It is an invitation to evil; and evil is sure to enter in and fill the unfurnished lodgings. And when, and how, you will get the evil lodgers out, none but God can tell.

3. There is yet another character, wiser, better far, but still failing to get the good of its ardour; which, because it knows its own ardency and its danger, deliberately chooses what is called monotony. But the monotony is not chosen only for the sake of safety (though that element does enter into the decision); nor is it chosen in the midst of idleness and drifting. These characters dread excitement, and with good reason, for they know not whither they may be carried! Now and again they taste excitement, and the taste pleases while it terrifies. They know what would be the pleasure of the gale and the rushing voyage, but they cling the more to harbour. "Let me always keep my anchor down," they say, "and my sails furled; were I to lift the anchor, and spread the sail, were the wind from the land to blow joyously, and fill the sail, I could not resist the freshening blast, I should forget all things for the sea. Therefore, I rest in my place. The wind may blow, but I will never unfurl the sail. Yet I will not rest in idleness. I will find things to do, and think, and feel. I will work for men and women, and help them through life; I will make the lives of others bright; I will crowd the day from end to end with labour; I know the laws which regulate my life, and I will obey them. Though my ship is at anchor, I will visit every other ship in the harbour, and bring them what good I can; I will receive into my ship all that come and give them all I can—always provided nothing I do, or say, or feel, puts a light to the pile of firewood in the heart of

the ship; for, once kindled, **it would** blaze **as high as heaven."**

This is good, so far as **it goes, and many a fervent heart** lives by this effort to the end **in useful security.** But such a life has, first, its own danger ; and, secondly, **it** is hampered by the repression of its most living qualities.

(1) It has its danger, for there is always **danger—no** matter how much work you may give yourself—if **you leave** one part of your nature unsatisfied. Its hunger and thirst may become, you cannot tell when, too great to be borne ; and hunger and thirst, in their extremes, do not reason, or wait, but rush upon **their** food. You have no business **to** make life wholly monotonous even though it be the monotony of work, for the power **in you** which hates monotony will burst through its barriers, unless you give it something to think of, to love, and to act upon. **It is too** perilous for you to live always in the common-place ; and work done only for duty's sake, **and not** with **joy, and** charm, and passion in it, is good for others, **but it is not** enough for you. And since it is not enough, **it has these** dangers. They may never come, but they are there.

(2) There is another mistake in this life. It has but little joy, and less excitement **in** its work. Nay, it keeps the work, by choice, monotonous. It does not allow too much feeling, too much fervour ; it keeps within the limits of the excellent commonplace ; nay, it strives to love the common-place, and says that it needs no **special joy,** for joy would make it discontented with the sober corn and oil of life. " Here, **in my** daily round and common task, among the old and the well-known, here I will abide and be content ; I

know it is monotonous; I know it is not enchanted land; but I will expect and seek no more."

Yes, that is very well if it could always be. But the soul that says it, regrets it while it says it; and the time will come—because it has crushed, and not exalted, the fervent quality which God gave it to use—when it will pity itself, and feel that half of life has gone to waste, that all has not been made of the nature given by God; and—the self-pity will be true. For when the heart is capable of joy, it ought to find joy—pure and noble joy, but still joy; not the pale shadow of it alone that the choosers of monotonous work make believe that they possess. When the soul is capable of fine and high excitement—that excitement for fitly beautiful and glorious things which kindles every feeling into swift life and into rapidity of action that stimulates others—it falls below itself when it never realizes that of which it is capable. When the soul *can* shape its ideals, it is sure—if it does not try to shape them, to have the rapture of creating, and of kindling others through creation —to seek and find unworthiness, and to realize it. To lose these things and their powers in a life which selects work which is monotonous—work which is not loved with joy, but done through dim fear, or through a sense of law alone, or to escape from a more drear monotony, or to hide oneself from thought, or to occupy the room of feeling—is to lose the greater and the nobler half of yourself. You were made to live the life of the lark, half your time singing at Heaven's gate in joy that gives joy to all the world beneath, and half your time in the joy of the nest below— and you have chosen the life of the barn-door fowl—

excellent, but not all you might have been. And the end is, that one day you will say, with infinite self-pity, and those who know you will think it pitiful also—"I am not myself: I never have been myself. Half the world I have within is barren rock, and it might have been covered with woods and wild flowers, and musical with streams. I have been useful, but I have been mechanical, and I fear that mechanical toil gives no impulse to others. I have, I trust, done good to men, but I am not sure. I have not loved my work with my whole heart, and the want of ardour in it, ardour of love, has prevented it from kindling others. He only who is aflame, inflames."

This is a sorrowful ending. And its worst sorrow is when life, in that sorrow, becomes like a frozen lake: glittering, having its own beauty, but smooth and cold. The living soul is, indeed, deep down beneath where the waters are not frozen, but there is no chance any more on earth of the warm waves breaking through! At last, death comes, and the ice-covered soul is let loose.

All these ways of meeting the dangers and the difficulties of an ardent spirit either wholly fail, or only partly succeed; and they fail because they one and all strive to crush, ignore, or leave uneducated an integral part of character. Natural character cannot be crushed: if you try to crush it, it avenges itself in the end, and out of that comes your punishment. But it can be recognized, accepted, and nobly developed. And in that method lies your true salvation. You can be fervent in spirit—and serving the Lord.

And now that I have described those quiet characters to whom monotonous life is natural, and who need to bring forth into life and nourish such seeds of fervour as may lie hid within them—and those who being fervent choose the monotonous life, but within whom hidden ardour flings its trailers as wildly as the woodbine—it is time to inquire what kind is the self-education which both these types of character, whose outward life is similar, are bound to give themselves. What are they to do?

One principle is enough to lay down at present. There is nothing in human nature which ought to be neglected, imprisoned, despised, or enslaved; no matter what dangers it may threaten, or what trouble it may give you; and if you attempt this kind of work, there will be rebellion: the enslaved or repressed quality will revolt and claim its rights. You may then crush it out, but what have you done? You have maimed yourself. Least of all, is ardour, fervency of nature, to be beaten down. For it is the quality which, nobly trained, gives life and beauty to all the rest.

That is the negative declaration of the principle. The positive form of it is this: Every quality of human nature—and among these none is nobler than ardour of heart—is not to be allowed to run wild like a street Arab—but to be reverenced, and used as a trust and gift from God; and, therefore, to be educated, taught its methods, developed into perfection through self-temperance; trained to do its own special work within those limits in which it grows most nobly and swiftly; made to see that its highest aim is not to please itself, but to be a helper of the other qualities, in order that, altogether, the whole assemblage of them may serve God, and do good to man; wrought into a free and loving servant of a righteous will; and every fibre of it supplied with food so that it may reach its full power and do its full work. It is not restraint then that fervour of spirit originally wants; it is high, loving, righteous, and active development. That is the principle, and it is contained in the words of the Apostle: "Fervent in spirit; serving the Lord."

[February 18, 1883.]

THE EDUCATION OF FERVOUR OF SPIRIT.

"Fervent in spirit; serving the Lord."—ROMANS xii. 11.

I HAVE spoken of the dangers which beset the quiet in spirit from their tendency to apathy; and of those which beset the fervent in spirit from their endeavour to imprison their fervour, or to let it loose without restraint; and I said that I would try to show how these dangers could be dispersed or changed. The same principle is valid for both, though the quiet spirit will apply it in one way, and the fervent in another.

That principle is this:—No natural quality is to be repressed, but is to be educated. It is not by coercion, but by the development into fulness of being of every essential quality of our nature that we can govern justly the little republic within us. Therefore, I say to those who love the quiet life—Give your nature liberty, let quietude have her perfect work; but if it run towards evil—that is, towards apathy or sloth—meet that difficulty, not by checking the quality itself, but by educating other powers in your nature which will balance it, and which, being developed, will strengthen and ennoble quietude. Apathy, sloth are really quietude weakened, not developed; quietude changing into helplessness, not rising into intelligence of itself, and into capacity for using its powers.

The true method of action has a different result.

There is sure to be, in all quiet natures, a little ardour somewhere; a capacity, however small, for strong loving and impassioned action at some one point; a power of aspiration, and for eager pursuit after at least one ideal. This undeveloped power may be hid in some recess within your soul, but if you seek for it you will find it. Bring the shy thing forth; put it into situations in which it must speak, must act; encourage it to love and to be eager; find out what aspiration kindles it, what ideal excites it—and develop it. This will give you some trouble, for the quiet man is naturally lazy, and his first failures are likely to induce what he calls despair; but half the happiness of your manhood depends on your making some exertion of this kind; and all the noble happiness of your old age.

The moment this little quality, now roused into activity, begins to move within you, its action will modify your quietude, and supply it with exactly that companion, which, without lessening its good, will hinder it from ever sliding into sloth, or drowning itself in apathy.

2. The same method is to be used with regard to fervour of spirit. Do not be ashamed of it, do not repress it so that it shall not speak; give it free course; set it to breathe the full air of heaven where it may act and glow. But lest it should lead you into danger, search for those qualities in you which will modify and ennoble its actions. There is sure to be somewhere in you some love of quietude, of the fair and gentle things which grow out of calm, and are only to be enjoyed in calm. Educate and give food to these qualities. They will not imprison or silence ardour, but they

will, by living with it, add to its life such elements as will soften its wildness, and set bounds to its extravagance.

There is sure to be also in you some love of temperance, of that noble quality which is the girdle of all the virtues. Indeed, the extravagance into which ardour often runs, suggests and creates, in hours of exhaustion, the desire and the reality of temperance. Develop this quality; make it one of the powers of the soul; be watchful till it is possessed; and then temperance, living side by side with ardour, will not, as you might think, lessen the heat of ardour, but increase it through concentration. Heat will not be dissipated, and is never dissipated by temperance in the things done. It is made white hot. And the work which is done by ardour married to temperance is the most suggestive, the most kindling, and the loveliest which is accomplished, in the arts, in politics, in science, in social movements, and in religion. In this way it will happen that instead of having crushed or lost the use and power of a fervent heart, you will have gained both quietude and activity, enthusiasm and calm; gained, that is, the full use of two powers, and developed both—for ardour is deepened by temperance, and temperance is kept warm by ardour.

Therefore I repeat the principle. It is not coercion of qualities which saves us from their dangerous extremes; it is the full development of *all* the qualities in the character. Each will then check the extravagant and erring growths of each, and minister to the right and beautiful growth of each; so that, at last, all the powers of the character, working in and through each other with full force, and charioted by ardour and temperance, race forwards to the last and highest goal—the perfection of the man in God.

That is the first principle of the education of a fervent nature. The second thing to be spoken of is the education itself. Every quality—and especially ardour which is the inspirer of the other qualities—needs more than the influence which the development of other qualities exercise upon it. It needs an education of its own. What, then, is the quiet soul which seeks ardour because it fears apathy, and the fervent soul which must ennoble ardour lest it should run away with its possessor—what are they to do? How is ardour of heart to be gained and trained?

i. Well, first, there are certain things which never grow old, never decay, and are always full of life; they are as beautiful in this century as they were a hundred centuries ago. These are the common things of earth and air, and the universal things of simple human nature—the loveliness of the woods and skies, the hills and waters, of the grass of the field, and the ways of animals and plants; the sweetness of human love and faith, the common duties and hopes and works of life; the universal relations, in purity and tenderness, of men to women, and women to men; the multitudinous interchanges of work, sympathy, sacrifice and help which pass between us all, hour by hour—multitudinous as the stars, and as beautiful; as constant in their companionship as sun and moon, and yet as everlasting. "Their sound is gone forth into all lands, and their words to the end of the world."

These are the things which men and women possess, but do not set themselves to love. They are thought to be too common; and as culture increases and curiosity develops, men seek for the strange and the uncommon, for the rare and the complex, on which to expand their ardour, and by which to awaken it. So grows up a life which, like our modern life, is full of failure, and full of exhaustion; for few can win the uncommon, and when it is won, it is soon drained dry.

But it should not be so with you. The simplicities of life are perennial streams. Live in your cottage by their side, and their sweet flowing will be the good and beauty of all your days.

It is not difficult for youth, and it should not be difficult for those who are older, to win the power of enjoying these simple and common things of nature and of life; to get out of them enchantment, such enchantment as the child has in its little garden; and by living with them daily to learn to love them with a love which never can grow cold. It is by companying with them, with set desire to keep and to encourage the natural joy and love with which they are at first attended, that the natural joy and love is exalted into an eternal and spiritual possession. Then as years go on, admiration of their beauty and power develops, for the more we know of them the wider seems their universe; and after admiration comes reverence of them, for we become conscious of their universality, their eternity, and that God is nearest to us in them. Out of all these, and continuously, stream the sources and the river of ardour. The quiet soul can find enough in them to kindle fervour, the stillest of mankind who has loved them can never pass into the apathetic life. The fiery heart who has gained them will not care to send its desires forth to strange lands, or to pursue strange excitements. It has enough, for its love and joy are full; and its passion is kept from wrong by noble admiration, by sacred reverence for their deathless and righteous beauty.

Nor are these words too strong. The simple things of nature and mankind are in truth the divine and beautiful things. The complex and curious things are not divine, for they are not purely human; not perfectly beautiful for they are exhaustible. As we penetrate into these common things of nature and man, as we go on living with them, they grow brighter and brighter, more and more varied. As we penetrate into and live with the remoter and difficult things, they grow wearisome, less and less varied. There is as much difference between the strange and sensational scenery of nature and human life, in which a diseased ardour loves to roam, and their original and simple elements, as there is between an artificial garden full of exotic flowers and the gracious universality of the grass of the field. The garden is but rarely seen, and we tire of it in a month. The grass spreads everywhere in soft and satisfying beauty; and in every place—beneath the trees, among the rocks, beside the stream, in nooks of the hills, on far-spread plains, in narrowing combes—is always different, and yet in difference is lovely. It is so with simple things, and with their joy and love. Once we have found their love, once we can enjoy them—our ardour for them, and the reasons of that ardour, grow day by day. And age, even in decay, keeps to them as fervent a spirit as youth, in its brightness and life, bestowed upon them. This then is one form of the education we should give to fervour of spirit. It is an education that guards our ardour from wrong, establishes it in good, preserves it and deepens it to the close of life.

ii. But this is not enough. We want something more upon which to feed ardour of heart than the every-day beauty of nature, and the every-day life and love of human life. We need to give the soul that which lifts us above the daily world, which enables us to soar and sing, which kindles in us that which seeks perfection, which aspires to see the " light that never was on sea or land." And this is now easy. For having attained to love of the simple and the common, we can now find the sublime and the imaginative. The first and the right step has been made, and in the true order. "First the natural, afterward that which is spiritual." It is through the real that we are made conscious of the ideal. It is when we are kindled by the daily beauty of the world, and thrilled by it, that there steals slowly into us—as often you must have felt in solitary places in the woods, or hills, or by the deep sea—a sense of something greater—of sublimity which cannot be expressed ; of universal life ; of thought that may not be circumscribed ; of love that is as a spiritual fire in all things ; of an infinite beauty, of which all beauty of air and earth is but the form. In such moments outward nature vanishes away, and we seem to stand alone, uplifted in silent and solemn awe, hand in hand with the invisible and everlasting God.

There are those who throw these hours and their emotions away as unfitted for practical life. I ask you to seize on them, to make their memories, when they themselves pass away, the favoured haunts of the imagination, to cherish them as the consecrated holidays of life ; to make them the food of the thoughts that kindle feeling in youth, and of the feelings which supply thought to age. Ardour of heart thrives upon them; grows into beauty through them, develops by them delicately and strongly; is ennobled by their company. They break into poetry in youth, they dedicate the beginning of manhood to high aims; they keep middle age free from the curse of worldliness, from the deceitfulness of riches, from overcare and overwork; and they are the exalting companions of old age. Educate your ardour with them, be borne with joy and rapture on their wings into the impassioned world of the imagination, into the infinite world where the spirit is alone with God. There will be no danger, with such companions, of exhausting ardour, no risk of rushing into extravagance; the spirit will be filled with a divine glow which will take earthly ardour into itself, and there exalt and purify it.

iii. Nearer to us, and more magnificent, are those ideals which come to us through the simple and common things of human life. We see with pleasure the gay, unconscious joy of children—and all in a moment we think of the perfect joy. We watch the love which binds two together, and makes the whole world romance to them—why is it that we pass beyond it to think of love for ever undivided, of a land where nothing shall grow old? We see, in the midst of sorrow and pain, one who daily surrenders life for love's sake, and finds in the surrender happiness—and through the sight we pass beyond it, and see the absolute sacrifice of which it is one form. We hear the story of the Prodigal Son—and it is not only a single forgiveness on earth we realize, but the universal forgiving of the Everlasting Father. We touch one instance of mercy, or gentleness, or long suffering—and how is it that we find ourselves enthralled by the sense of their eternal beauty? We rejoice, finding one example of righteousness and purity won through moral strife or faith in God—and are carried forward as if on wings to behold the face of absolute righteousness. We are excited by some pursuit of truth which has ended in grasping the truth; by some struggle for liberty which has won its day, or its crown of martyrdom; by some endeavour towards one form of beauty which has at last shaped itself in music or in art;—and it is impossible to stay in any of these things: we leave them behind, and for the moment (but through their impulse) realize the divine labour which rejoices as it creates, absolute truth and the knowledge of it, liberty found by all the world of men and sanctioned by the decree of God; beauty ever flowing, always perfect, and accomplishing itself in a myriad-formed variety. So, through the natural and common things of man, we conceive in a just way their ideals; and, conceiving them, love them with joy unspeakable and full of glory. Yes, these are ideas: they make the high clear air into which we can mount and sing when we leave our nest below. While we fly upwards in them, we know what we shall be when we see God as He is.

These ideas, then, are the ethereal food of ardour. For them I bid you burn and glow. They lead to no monotony; they cannot be exhausted. There is no extravagance in their enthusiasm; no sin or wrong hidden behind their beauty, and of their noble pursuit there is no end; and in it no shipwreck. Tongue cannot tell what a life it is to live within them, and what a death it is which dies expecting clearer vision of them.

But it is not enough to **glow only within** with these ideas. Indeed, if you have them truly, and burn with them, they **force you** into activity. Therefore, would you still further **feed** and educate ardour of heart, live **for these ideas as** Christ your Master lived for them? Let **the fire of them pass from** thoughts and feelings into acts; kindle **others by** shaping their light and heat within you into deeds **before** men, and for the sake of men. Show forth, as beautifully as you can, the ideals in reality, so that men may be lured to run after them. **Make** clear your ardent love of **love, of** truth, **of** liberty, of forgiveness, and **of** beauty, by living and dying for it. Sacrifice your whole life upon its altar **with a fervent and** willing heart. Then you will understand what the **Son of** Man—who thus lived, and in such ardour —meant when He said, "I, if be lifted up, will draw all men to me."

iv. Then—there is yet another step. Ask yourselves —Are these things only ideas, **or do they inhere in one** Being, **from** whom they come to us, and in whom they **are** essential and perfect, and, therefore, most blessed **of all** tidings, in union with whom we shall realize their perfect beauty?

And the answer to **that** question is **a rejoicing** affirmative. There *is* God—our **Father.** This **is** the answer Jesus Christ gave, "Be ye **therefore perfect;** even as your Father **which** is in heaven is **perfect."** All the daily beauty of **earth,** and air, **and human** life, and all the ideals **of** mankind **flow** from Him, are made in Him, *are* Himself;

are absolute in perfection in Him. When, therefore, we burn and glow for them, we burn and glow for God. To know that truth, to realize it as the deepest foundation of life, is to make all life religious.

Then—in this ordered progress of the education of ardour—we have reached the goal, the highest worship which fervour of spirit can give; the celestial food by which it lives most purely, nobly, and eternally; the home where ardour flames for ever, but also is at peace for ever.

Lastly, in this wisely-regulated life, has not the possibility of the evils, dangers, and unwisdom of which I spoke disappeared? They cannot come to quietude which has sought such ardour, or to ardour which has undergone this education. The passion of goodness is at the root of daily life; the passion for perfection at the root of imaginative life; and the love of God, as of a child to a father, carries both onwards for ever into the eternal world. Nor is the present lost; for in it all the simple things we first love are preserved. The higher ardours have grown out of the lower, as naturally as the branches of a tree from its root and stem; and they, taking from the light and air of heaven new energy, send it back to the roots of common life, so that they also multiply themselves, and strike more deeply, firmly, and with greater joy, into the simple and natural humanity, out of which at first the tree arose. The real, the ideal, and God, are knit each to each in natural piety; we lose ourselves; and, bathed in one glowing ardour of love and joy, are, at last—fervent in spirit, and at one with God.

[February 25, 1883.]

YOUTH.—FERVENT IN SPIRIT.

"Not slothful in business; fervent in spirit; serving the Lord."—ROMANS xii. 11.

THE sermons I have preached on this text have been chiefly occupied in analysis of certain forms of feeling and act belonging to a fervent heart, and with the manner of avoiding the dangers and educating the capacities which belong to it. What has been said, therefore, has chiefly belonged to the inner life. Of that portion of the text which belongs to the outer life—"slothful in business"—nothing has yet been said; and of its latter clause—"serving the Lord"—not enough has yet been said.

The three phrases may be allotted to the three periods of life—to youth, to middle age, and to old age. It is natural that fervour of heart should rule in youth; that activity in business should rule in manhood; that serving the Lord should have the undivided attention of old age. But when I say that these several things rule in each period, I do not mean that youth should not serve the Lord and be active in business; that middle age should not be fervent in spirit and serve the Lord; that age should not be eager of heart and active in its own work—but only that at each of these periods one of these aims or qualities of heart has naturally the most attention given to it. It is the mistake of life that so many men act as if they said, "I will be ardent only in youth; active only in manhood; I will serve God only in old age." That is common, and common is the result—the loss in manhood of the powers of youth, because all its fervour, being unbalanced, has been exhausted; the incapacity of manhood for perfect development, because it is given up to business only; and when old age comes, inability to serve the Lord, for the man can scarcely hope to take up when he is decaying that which he has neglected all his life. I will, therefore, speak to-day of how youth should, in the midst of its fervour, be not slothful in business, and how it should serve the Lord.

Youth is the time when feeling is most awake, and most enjoys itself. The freshness of its morning is like sunlight in all things, and every day opens a new land to curiosity, to effort, and to joy. We love the beauty of the world, and do not spoil the beauty by asking how or why we love it. It is for that reason that hour by hour revelations are made to us by nature, that we live upon the crest of enjoyment, always fervent for the future. Nor is our life with man less wonderful, less impassioned. Keen in our sympathy for the rights of man, we are as keen in our indignation against his wrongs. We play with every theory that concerns the progress of the race, have daily dreams of what we will do for it, look forward to a golden age and sing it; spend an infinity of emotion on the past history, on the present struggles, and have an infinite faith in the future, of mankind. Personal love adds its passion to universal love and deepens our capacity of feeling; and with first love come ideal dreams—those visions which form so much of the scenery of youth, and which, though they may never be realized, are yet the fountain by whose waters the whole of life is sweetened, ennobled, and kept pure.

Youth should be full of beauty, joy and fervour; and it is one of the worst curses of a conventional society that so few have any youth at all. How many of the young men and young girls whom we meet are fervent in spirit? Tied up like plants in a greenhouse, they are clipped into the shapes that society imposes on them, and their fate is to produce a multitude of over-developed flowers at a certain time, and then—so far as blossoming or beauty, fervour or natural impulse are concerned—to be no more good at all for the rest of their lives.

But you who do feel, enjoy, and love naturally, and who are eager to put aside conventionalities when they limit that which is natural and simple and true, let your youth and all it has possess their fulness. As long as you are children of the bridechamber, do not fast. But remember that life is not all youth, and that the way ahead is long. Noon is coming with its burning heat, and afternoon, and evening—and the fervent heart is not all you need with which to meet these later days of life. Unless you have strengthened and ennobled the qualities of youth, they will be exhausted while you are yet young, and manhood and old age will be defrauded of their use and presence.

How, then, are you to prepare in youth to meet the trials of manhood and old age, to strengthen and develop those special qualities of youth which you ought to carry with you, as powers of the soul, into later life? Bring into youth the special needs and powers of after life. Let it be not slothful in business, and let it serve the Lord.

i. *Not slothful in business.* Unless you gain in youth the habit of work, you will have to dedicate all the first years of manhood to gaining it, and all the time you then spend in winning with difficulty what you ought to have already won with ease is dead loss which you might have avoided, and which you never can replace. I do not say that you are to work so as to lose joy, excitement, love, for then you will ruin your youth and spoil your manhood, but you must bring work into your joy and love. How? There is the delight you have in Nature: mingle with it some knowledge! Get some ideas with regard to the causes of the things you love! It will not make the way of the winds with the clouds less beautiful when you take some trouble to know how they move and why they are so lovely. It will not make the earth less glorious if you know, by some steady labour, how the hills were built and hewn into the forms that kindle in you poetic feeling. And you will have gained a power beyond the knowledge and beyond the feeling which you can use like a sword in after life to open your way through the world.

Let it be the same with your impassioned desires for man and with your personal love and ideals. Find out some way, even the slightest, by which day by day you may put your enthusiasm into a practical form, and cling close to the doing of this little thing until you bring it into finish. Do not begin another thing till that one thing is in working order. That will give you power. He who can finish that which is least can finish, in after life, that which is greatest. And as to your excitement and its youthful joy—instead of being lessened it will be doubled. Nothing increases excitement of a true kind so much as putting that about which we are excited into working form. The same is true with regard to ideals. You have a vision of absolute self-sacrifice, of universal justice. Well, keep the visions; let them illuminate and glorify life, but be not slothful in their business. All ideals have their work, or they cease to be ideals. Sacrifice yourself for others—here, at home; sacrifice your poetic contemplation of self-sacrifice for the sake of making a brother, a sister, a friend happier—get the ideal of love into some form. The dream of universal justice and truth is beautiful, but it will pass away if you are not active about it. Take some pains, then, to be just and truthful in the particular; for the proper food of universal ideals is particular practice of them. If you want justice all over the world—be just in your own little corner of it. Get, I say again, the ideal into form and with activity, and you will find that you will lose nothing of your delight in the imaginative vision, nor will the vision become less beautiful. On the contrary, the ideal will grow more splendid; the vision open new worlds to you, your fervour increase, and your youth have more rapture.

As to personal love, it is the same. The days of first love, all the days of youthful love, are enchanting. It is a business in which one is never slothful; but it is often a time when we are lured into doing no other business; and, through that, a foundation of laziness is laid for life. Drifting and idleness become habits of the soul, and, by and by, when love has had its way and won its goal, we who have been most romantic, most fervent, are surprised in after life, when we look back to find that all the romance is gone, all the fervour grown cold; and though love has remained true, yet that it has become commonplace. It wears no more its robe of many colours, nor does the sunshine fall upon it now, or the glow of imagination. Its charm has been left behind in the fields of youth. This is a common story, and a sad one. Of all sorrowful things the death of romance is the most sorrowful.

One reason of this sad thing is that love has not been united to any other activity, to any other interest or business than its own. It ought to have taken into its house—" Not slothful in business." Love, when it is of the best quality, should not only be full of itself, but should kindle and stimulate all the powers of life; should make you conscious of powers you did not know of, and never let you rest until you had used them; should make you do all the things you have to do much better than before; think twice as quickly, act with double swiftness; live with more truth, more faith, more hope, more of purpose than before; set every capacity into movement; make every beautiful thing more beautiful, and every ideal more ideal, and your desire to get the beautiful into form, and the ideal into some reality, so intense that you cannot rest until you are accomplishing your desire.

That is what love should do; make you not only not slothful in its own work, but not slothful in the business of life. And then—what happens? Has love lessened through this activity beyond itself? Is it made less ideal, less romantic, when its power is used for the practical work of life, for realities? Is it less concentrated on its object because its strength is spread abroad over many interests, or less beautiful because it is taken into the midst of the commonplace? No, indeed; it is increased, because all the interests in which it has shared have poured each their additional interest into it; it is more romantic, more ideal more enkindled, and more beautiful, because it has proved its power to shed romance over the commonplace, to make the everyday things of life ideal, to change the slowest work into the swiftest, and the ugliest work into beauty and splendour; until this mutual and enlivening action of love and of activity upon each other, this doubling and trebling of life, moving together over a hundred interests—are all taken, with all their powers, and added to love and to the object loved, so that concentration of feeling is increased by expansion of feeling, and personal love made tenfold more profound and fervent because more living, more excited, and more interesting.

And after-life knows the blessing of that earnest effort to realize the ideal. Love so wrought together with activity, so divided from slothfulness, so expanded over all the world, does not decay, does not lose its beauty, its changeful coat, its sunshine of imagination, its romance. Accustomed from the beginning to movement, it is always alive. Trained to use its power in work, all the interest of afterwork naturally flows into it, and is part of its sweet waters. The charm is kept, love's memories of the past are always sweet, its future always ideal, its present always tender.

That is a work well worthy of youth to do; and it

is done by adding the special aim of manhood, "activity in business," to the special quality of youth, "fervour of heart." On this, then, I have said enough. The principle is now easily grasped, and each may apply it as they please.

But this is only a part of what I have to say. We must bring into youth and its fervour, not only the activity of manhood, but the religious spirit which ought to be deepest in old age. *In youth let us serve the Lord.* Not as in age, not in the same way as in manhood—to each their own—but in the way that fits the time.

There are those who do not care to bring God into their youth, who are content with its joy and live only from hour to hour. It is time enough, they think, to seek for their Father when trouble comes in later life, or when death is coming in age. It is *not* time enough. When we have not known our God as the Giver of our joy, we shall not easily be able to see Him as our Father in the darkness of manhood's trouble, and love Him through our trial, and have His power with us for our battle. We are more likely then to think Him our enemy, to see our trouble as His wrath, and our weakness as His cruelty; and if death should come, to find it hard to know that behind death He is waiting, and that in death He is our life.

When we think only of God's anger, troubles continue, are deepened, and sever us farther from Him; nor does death bring us at once, with conscious joy, into His presence. No; that communion with God which makes the strength of manhood and the comfort of age and the life of death, is not to be gained in a moment, and ought to be rooted deep in the consecration of youth to His service. Give to God the freshness of your early inspiration. If He bestow upon you joy and fervour, activity and love, forget not the Giver in the gifts. Sanctify the brightness of youth with watchfulness against wrong, with carefulness for love and truth, with prayerful dedication of your inward life to the Father who loves you, with constant and conscious union of all your outward life to His will. And then when trouble comes, you will know His hand in it, and see His smile, and be thrilled with His power; and in death look upwards and behold the countenance of eternal life. Not in careless pleasure, but in watchful love and trust of God your Father, in faithful and fervent desire to be His child, is the secret of life's victory, and of the overcoming of death by life.

Others are not so much careless of serving the Lord, as steadily opposed to it. I do not say they hate religion, but they abjure it. They have no reverence for it; all worship wearies them; all emotion of it is mere sentiment, and not science; and God, they say, is but a name for their own ideas, and as their ideas are but a weakness, they bid them begone.

Well, they cannot be helped at present, for vanity has got hold of them. And they may live very well upon their vanity. It is a food which never fails, but it only feeds the possessor, and it will become in the end a great weariness to him, and is, indeed, always a weariness to others. I do not say that the root of this scorn or abjuration of God is vanity in those who in middle age or in later life throw God and religion away. *They* do it seriously, and often after long struggle and trouble; but when young people, who have had no experience in life, profess openly to cast God aside, it is almost always vanity, adoration of their own opinions, which prompt them to do so. And through their vanity they lose reverence and humility and the sense of things beyond them and above them, and their aspiration which they think they retain is not aspiration, it is ambition. They can succeed in winning a good place in the world, in getting wealth, in securing a moral reputation, in being admirable reasoners—but there is one thing in which they will not succeed. They will never be good artists in anything—only mechanicians in painting, poetry, and music —nor will they ever move, thrill, or inspire mankind. In manhood or womanhood they will never awaken a great love, or stir a great aspiration, or create a great ideal. They will set no one on fire. They have lost the use of youth in vanity, or in coldness of heart. If you tell them this, they will not believe it, indeed, they could not believe it, but it is true; and of all the piteous things of the present day, the most piteous is youth which boasts itself on being without a God. You may save those who are near this fate, if you are very wise and loving, but you cannot save those who are in it. It is one of those matters which has to be left to God Himself. But you who are young and not vain, do not lose the serving of God in your youth. Take all your fervour, all your joy in nature, all your love, all your ideals, and mingle with them worship and love of God.

There is your love of the natural world, your desire to penetrate its secrets. I have always said that we cannot realize God as personal in the universe or in its parts, but we can pass below the surface, and become conscious, through the conception of the whole, and then, through the vision of any part, of a vast Life moving in perfect order, of a Thought which is as vast as the life and which informs it, and then, of Love, as vast as life and thought and informing both, which kindles all this universe, and is that, which, when you discover a secret way of nature, makes your brain leap with joy; and that which, when you stand ravished in the woodland beauty or awed into solemn pleasure among the mountain storms, is flowing through you, and making you at one with itself. What is that life, thought, love? It is God the Lord. Take the mighty conception always with you. It is impersonal, but none the less real; and it will elevate all scientific work on nature, give a soul to all the doing of an artist, and double through its grandeur all poetic joy in nature. To keep it always with you is—in this sphere of youthful life—to serve the Lord.

Then, there is youthful love. When it comes, lay it at the feet of the Lord of all love. Let it be sanctified and hallowed, all through its course, with constant reference to Him who is righteousness, truth, faithfulness, purity, and gentleness. Thus, you will keep it free from self, free from sin, free from vanity, free from commonplace; and ennoble it, through your union with the eternal, with the glory of the Infinite. And God, realized now as caring for your love, and in sympathy with it, will begin to grow personal to you, and dear to you, and at home with you, as friend to friend. You will add the personal to the impersonal conception.

Then, again, there are all the ideals of youth and all its

dreams for man. It is in the belief that all these ideals are somewhere realized—that there is a perfect love, a perfect righteousness, actually thinking, feeling, and acting, and who will bring us finally to the level of our ideals in union with Himself—it is in that belief that the ideals of youth take consistency, win the power of inspiring act, and become, not visions which die in disappointment, but capacities and powers of the soul.

And as these deepen into powers, and our faith in their having a source in one mighty Being grows, we begin to see that the dreams we have had of the future of mankind are not merely the hopes of a poet, but the certainties of noble faith. For now we know that we all have come from God, and that He is in us, as He is in nature: personal with us because we are personal, impersonal in nature because nature is impersonal; and, therefore, that man can never be divided from Him. As sure as He lives, all men shall live for ever. As sure as He loves, all men shall love for ever. As sure as He is righteous, all that have streamed from Him, and taken personality, shall be personally righteous for evermore. To have that faith is to serve the Lord in youth, for all these beliefs, being living and impassionating thoughts, kindle the outward life into their own activities.

Slowly, then—and here is the end—there grows up in such a life the sense that we are knit to God, as a child to a Father (the sense in which personal religion of the heart begins); the feeling out of which grows personal love of God, passionate desire to do His holy will, and to be at one with Him for ever. The knowledge of a divine communion begins; and life is ennobled by it. The sense of eternity grows up within us, the faith in everlasting life. And, for this world, and for the next, there is now purpose in our life—the purpose of holiness, of union with God, of union with all men through Him—and with this purpose mingles the faith in everlasting joy for all mankind. These add their powers to the fervour and the activity of youth, and will flow through the whole of manhood into our old age. This is the serving of the Lord in youth. It is not yet what it will be; but it is enough for the time. The seed has been sown, the plant has shot above the ground, the spring airs are round it, and the sunshine of God feeds it. It will grow; the trials of after-life will not deform, but develop it; old age will not destroy its glory, but make it perfect.

[March 4, 1883.]

MIDDLE AGE.—NOT SLOTHFUL IN BUSINESS.

" Not slothful in business; fervent in spirit; serving the Lord."—
ROMANS xii. 11.

EVERY one who can be said to have lived has heard the cry—" not slothful in business "—on passing out of youth into manhood, on entering the world of men. The time had come when we knew we had to put preparation aside, and to do that for which we had prepared ourselves; when we heard the voice of home less and lessening, because the call was so loud which came to us from the world without; when the claim of mankind on our work was so powerful within, that we were forced to put aside dreams, ideals, love, and beauty, or at least our absorption in them, and go forth to answer—" I am here "—as a soldier in the ranks of human labour.

There are many who obey the call reluctantly, sulkily, slothfully, casting back longing looks to the garden in which they have lived; hating the waste land they are called on to reclaim, and the toil of reclaiming it still more; impatient as children with the thorns and thistles which spring up under their feet. But he who puts his hand to the plough and looks back is not fit for the kingdom of Labour, any more than he is fit for the kingdom of God. Whatever else ought to be true of us in manhood, there is one thing which is the foundation of all nobility of character—it is activity, "not slothful in business." And in this country most men are workers. There *is* an idle class who cumber the world and rob the state, and live by the overtoil of others; but I speak of the workers of the world, who give their whole middle-life to labour.

They do rightly; and I need not sing the praises of earnest and steady work which runs to its goal, and wins its goal; or runs to its goal, and seems to fail. Whether it win or fail, matters not, provided the work be good. Indeed, it is often the failures of honest work which are of most use to mankind. The torch which drops from the faithful hand is not extinguished. Another runner takes it up, and the work itself is done, though the first worker has died upon the way! And for himself the sorrow of his failure lasts but a little time. For the labourer lives again, and in the higher world rejoices that though he may be forgotten the work is done which he began. It is not personal success that God or man demand of us. It is that we be not slothful in what we undertake.

But this set life of work has its dangers, and especially at this time when many men seem to think work the only good. There are those who live for nothing else and think of nothing else; who are like horses harnessed in the morning to turn the monotonous mill, and who, unharnessed at night, eat and fall asleep to renew the same dreary toil day after day throughout the year. Or, tired of this, they plunge into speculation and are consumed with cares and fears about money. Or, having made their money, they rush into the other extreme of idleness and dissipation, and squander their wealth as fast as they have made it. Or, not having desire for either extreme of work or speculation, they settle down into a low life of weary care and weary labour, and creep to death all their days, over weighted with their own apathy. And with them all abides one idol, whose worship more than all else degrades and renders dead the soul—the idol of the world's opinion of their life; what their large or small society will say of them and of their work. That is their God; and a miserable fetish it is!

In such lives, then, what room is there for joy, for love of beauty, for love of noble musing, for seeing and hearing that which uplifts the soul; for the dreaming which puts them in mind of Paradise, for the ideals which take them out of themselves and make them think of man as a whole; for the wants of the spirit within them and the mighty hopes which take a man's hand and lead him up to God; which, in fruitful solitude and wise leisure, cause him to hear the voice—like John of Patmos—as it were of a trumpet talking to him and saying—" Come up hither, and I will show thee things that shall be hereafter." All their youth has perished; all its fervour, all its joy, all its sweet and high enchantment! The men have lost their wings; and, at times, the infinite pitifulness of this passes by them like a vision with bright hair, weeping and crying " Out upon them," and they know its wail is the cry of a loss they never can repair, and one hour of whose ancient gain were worth all their successful years. They have not been slothful in business, but they have been nothing else, and their life is ruined. This is the fate of thousands. It is not easy to be saved from it when once it has been accepted as a good, but I warn of it the young who are entering into the business of life. And the warning may be couched in words easy to remember—"Take care to bring into all work which you are not to do slothfully the fervour of spirit which chiefly belongs to youth, and the serving of the Lord which chiefly belongs to old age. Be not slothful in business, but also, through your manhood, be fervent in spirit, and serve the Lord.

Do not let the spirit of youth pass wholly away! In the midst of the great city's press of men, remember still the days when you loved the beauty of the woods and hills; and let the memory be dear, so dear that you cannot be content to live without renewing joys so pure. Lose some money, give some time, that you may refresh your eyes and restore your heart with the loveliness of nature which is given without price, but which will not give itself to a soul which thinks only of things that are given with price. Nor yet wholly surrender romance. Romance lies in the power of passionately feeling all things that are beautiful and noble in humanity, but chiefly all things that belong to love; and it pertains, as deeply, but in a different way, to the heart of the old man as it does to youth, and as it ought to do to manhood. Keep your soul alive to it in the midst of business. If intensity of work chill or decay that power in you, be sure you are losing that which you will miss most bitterly when old age steals upon you; and be still more sure then, that work and the worldliness it often brings with it are doing you grievous wrong. Better lose some prosperity, better give up some of your money and position than grow insensitive to kindling feeling, dull of heart, chill and half-dead within. Be not slothful in business, but keep romance of heart. Let youth run on into manhood.

Nor altogether lose your dreams, because they are unpractical; or forget your ideals, because you have not time to realize them. If you can no more look forward to a golden age for man; if you have lost all optimism, if you never dream as a poet dreams; if no visions come before you of glorious things which may yet happen to mankind; if you have no hopes or sorrows or sympathies beyond yourself, if you can never leave your own daily life and all its imprisoning interests, and lose yourself in prophecy—if you have no ideals, never see the ideal of perfect Truth, absolute Self-sacrifice, unstained Justice, Beauty without a flaw; if no aspiration towards the unattainable ever besets you or lifts you towards imaginative perfection; if all these things, which belong to youth and which live by fervour of spirit, have left you, because you are not slothful in business—then, your business is killing more than half of your true life; and, when age comes, you will not only be a half-dead, miserable man, but you will have lost those qualities without which you will not be able to serve the Lord in any faithful or noble way.

To live by these things alone in manhood would be folly. To carry youth only into manhood is never to be a man; but to take nothing of your ardent youth with you, is, in losing the continuity of personality, and in losing all inspiration, never to become a complete man.

ii. If these things are true with regard to ardour of heart mingled with activity of work, still more are they true with regard to serving God in the midst of unslothful business.

It has been too much the fashion to divide the service of God from the work of the world, to call on men to leave all business to follow Christ, as if Christ meant when he called Peter and Matthew away for a special missionary work, that no one should remain to do the needful works of life, and that no one who did not leave these works could follow him. Thus mistaking a particular call of special men to a particular work for a universal call to all men, the fatal division was made of sacred and profane work; as if any work was profane which was done in the spirit of Christ; as if Christ himself wished to make the whole of mankind into missionary preachers. To those who had that spirit he said—"Leave all—sell what you have—and come with me"—and wise advice it is. The mission preacher had better cling to his work, and leave all other work alone. Property and its duties are only his confusion. But Jesus had no such advice for those who had another kind of call. He did not bid the business man leave his business, but do it for the sake of man and in faith in God. The parable of the talents does not encourage flight from the work of the world.

The true teaching of Jesus was that all work was given to men by God, and was to be done divinely, with love and faith and joy. The true way to serve God in business is not to leave it for idleness of spiritual contemplation, but to do it in the faith that God Himself has sent you into the world to do it; and to reveal, through your doing of it, a part of His character to man. Whatever profession, trade, or craft you be, it is God Himself who has given you that work, and placed you there to serve Him in it. It is God's work you do; and He is in you doing it, for the sake of other men, His children. This is the faith which will save you from all wrong in your work, from worldliness in it, from selfishness in it; and make its highest aim, not your own wealth, or your own advance, but the manifestation in it of all that is God's character—of truth, justice, love, uprightness, reverence for the work itself so that it may be the very best you can do—and, beyond that, the ultimate direction of all that you do to the bettering, the development, and the saving of mankind. To show forth in work—in law, in medicine, in literature, in art, in the ministry, in all trades, in all handicrafts, in everything that man or woman can do—the character of God, and to direct all work to the advance and blessing of your brother-men; is to serve God while you are not slothful; and a sacred and beautiful conception it is of the business of middle age.

And when you have that faith and live by it, you will carry with you "through bustling lane and wrangling mart," through household cares and common duties, a secret sweetness, charm and grace, which will make life as fair and gracious as a summer's day. Amid the noise and overwhelming of the world, you will have in your heart the music of a divine communion; the comfort of your Father's love; and in your ears the tranquillizing voice of Jesus—"Let not your heart be troubled."

These are the powers of the soul which will lessen the temptations and guard you in the troubles of middle life.

They will lessen the temptations, because, carried with you into the midst of business, they, of their own power, make you careless of men's opinion, keep that villain, Worldliness, outside the doors of your heart; hinder the growth of the vanity of riches (vanity of hoarding them, vanity of expending them), keep at bay the tyranny of anxieties, the terror of losing property; and protect you from the weariness of labour and the loneliness of a life whose only care is to increase its store. Glorious and bright-eyed are these guests of the soul! They will save you from the ruin which falls on poor and rich alike who have been "not slothful in business," but have never been fervent in spirit, nor have served the Lord.

And then in trouble, as well as in temptation, you have these powers as your great allies.

Often in such trouble as illness, you are thrown out of work. If business be your all in all, what are you to do? There you lie, chafing on your couch, querulous because you miss your daily work, bored to death—a melancholy picture, and one that deserves but little pity, for it is your own fault. You have lost the powers of youth and not anticipated those of age. Had you kept the joy of love, the capacity for dreaming, the desire of beauty, the fervour of heart which inspires life, the passion of the ideal; had you in your soul some service of God, some desire to bless mankind with the love of Jesus Christ, do you think you would lie there complaining, more like a wounded animal than a man? Why, your life would be as full as if you were in the very express of business!

And the deeper troubles which beset the human heart, which, while we are driven to do our daily business, we carry with us at home or abroad, deep down within—the devourers of life—these finally kill if they are continued. Work only dulls them for a time, and through the day; they pierce with their hornet sting at night! Nor does work relieve them; and when they make it wearisome, and, in the end, cause us to do it badly, then work itself—being ill done, and we being conscious of its weakness—becomes a fresh trouble, and adds itself to the others. Then, when work has failed, what remains? Nothing; and the man burns out like a fire in a swift wind. I have seen it only too often!

But this is not the case if we have kept the powers of our youth. The memory of joy is in itself a joy—a refuge from pain, a shadow from the heat, a shelter as of a great rock in a weary land. The power of loving sustains a happiness in sorrow, and keeps us capable of hope. There is no trouble, we think, which may not be—if we bear it nobly—of use to the race of men; and in that outward thought we lose the overwhelming of self-thought, and pardon our pain in the knowledge that it will bring a good to man. The fervour in our heart upraises us above our torment; imagination opens to us her glorious world. We are cast down, but not destroyed. We live on, and win out of trouble into sunny life again.

Still less does trouble overwhelm us if we have faith in God. Always in our ears are the words of Christ—"In this world ye shall have tribulation, but be of good cheer, I have overcome the world."

Our trouble is in God's will, and it is His will that we should despise its power to subdue the soul—extract its power to develop the soul. All trouble has its need in the mind of God. It is to do some good, to bring some power to others, to ennoble or to make happier some who are ignoble or unhappy. "My God," we then cry, "take me—use me for mankind! Give me Thy companionship, that I may bear, work through, and conquer all the evil in my sorrow! Give me love, that I may make my pain into the power of help!"

He who can so believe and so love is not beaten in the midst of business by any pain whatever.

Finally, business power is not lessened in this life. Nay, it is increased. Fervour of heart will stimulate all your powers. Your intellect will be quicker to do the work of the world, and your mind, through the penetration of the heart, more fitted to discover men who can be your helpers. A finer imagination will discover more fields of business, and you will expand your work. The dreams and ideals you possess will ennoble your business, and make it delightful. It will take into it so high a thought and so profound a feeling, when it takes into it as an end the bettering and progress of man, that it can never become a weariness, nor you be ever solitary in it. You will be bright, uplifted, at rest, and capable of joy, even to the end.

And God will bless your work with the power of bestowing pleasure, because it is done, not for yourself alone, but for the use and joy and growth of all His children; and the blessing will fall back upon your own heart and make you happy. And happiness within—is not that the climate in which business is least slothful, done in the finest fashion, finished—because of the pleasure in it—to the remotest fibre, polished to the nail?

This is the life I lay before you. It is true you will make less money; you may not reach the social height others reach; the world of society and of wealth may not court you; but all the question lies in this—what is a man's life? Is it in the things he possesses, or is it in what he is? Is it in having money and fame and the approval of the world or is it in joy, in beauty, in imagination's world, in the love of mankind and the power of loving, in a heart at peace, in the companionship of God, in the life of Jesus Christ, in the spirit which can rejoice to say, "I wish to live and love for ever"?

[March 11, 1883.]

OLD AGE.—SERVING THE LORD.

"Not slothful in business; fervent in spirit; serving the Lord."—
ROMANS xii. 11.

OUR text has been concerned with three periods of life, with their special powers and work. Of youth and its fervour we have spoken, of middle-age and its activity. Our subject now is old age and its special service of the Lord. But the principle laid down did not assert that in old age alone we were to serve the Lord, or that in old age we could not be active or fervent in spirit. On the contrary, it averred that while each period had a pre-eminent aim of its own, it could not develop it in the best possible way unless the pre-eminent interests of the two other periods were taken into it; nay, more, that youth, manhood, and old age were each incomplete and even fruitless, unless the powers of the three were bound together.

When youth passed away, its special pleasures, its outward manners and work passed with it. But if it had brought down into its life some of the serious activity which belongs to manhood, and something of the quiet consecration of old age to the service of the Lord; then—though its outward elements were left behind—all that was enduring in its fervour passed on into manhood, and became in the midst of its unslothful activity a spirit of life, aspiration and love which guarded heavy labour from many dangers. But manhood, thus preserving what was best in youth, was not content with that alone; it borrowed from old age the special aim of old age; it hallowed all its business with that serving of the Lord which makes business not a serving of self, but a service of mankind. And this was easy in manhood, because the serving of the Lord had begun in youth and was supported through manhood by the unselfish ardour of youth.

So now, when age has come and the excitement of youth is long gone by, and business has been laid aside, the serving of the Lord, the purpose and delight of age, is not difficult to accomplish strongly or to feel passionately. It is no sudden thing taken up in a moment; it has begun where the stream of life rushed forth, on the hills of childhood, and kept company with the waters as they sprang from rock to rock in the gladness of their youth. It went with the river when it flowed, a fuller and a fuller tide, through the fertile meadows and past the busy towns of manhood. It is with old age still, its most beloved companion, as slowly flowing, but deep and full, it nears the ocean of eternity. The habit of life has been to serve the Lord, and now the time has come for the fulfilled development of this service; it takes the foremost place in the finishing of life.

But the service of God does not stand alone in old age. The spirit of the ardour of youth has been carried into manhood; it is still borne onward into old age. Nor does the activity of manhood, idealized by the ardour of youth, die with the dying of the work of manhood. It, too, is carried into old age. It is then that old age is perfect. Old age is not the decaying of the man; it is his highest reach on earth; the completion of all periods in one, the crown of life. This is the fine doctrine of continuity—the historical continuity of personality; each period of life knit to each, the powers and practice, the thoughts and feelings of each time woven in and through one another, so that the growth is as natural, as successive, as steady, as beautiful and as finished as the growth of a great tree.

These are the things to be expanded. And first take the contrast. Look at old age which has come on a man when none of this previous work has been done.

I described what manhood was when all that belonged to youth had been squandered, so that none of youth's fine spirit was carried on into the graver activities of middle age—a manhood subject to the transient world, worshipping the idol of wealth, enslaved by dreary cares, corrupted with work which turns into a disease; without the joy of love, abandoned of romance, undone of dreams, having no ideals, disbelieving in aspirations; successful without, ruined within; and when old age touches it, exhausted.

What kind of an old age is that which follows? It has none of the spirit of youth in it. The man hates his old age, and hates it all the more when he remembers his youth: for he thinks how much he hoped for, how passionately he wrought and felt, how eager was his love, how high were his ideals, how bright were the wings of joy on which he was borne along. And now—it is all gone! Not one trace of it remains within; not one ray of it is shining on his heart. And as his nature is either stern or soft, so does he turn in age to fruitless scorn or to fruitless sorrow—sour scorn of the ancient time when he believed and loved and dreamed—for has it not all proved false, is it not all outworn, all turned into evil?

> "Virtue! to be good and just!
> Every heart when sifted well,
> Is a clot of warmer dust
> Mixed with cunning sparks of hell."

Or, it is not scorn, but bitter and miserable sorrow to feel that all is gone by, save vain regrets, vain longing for the swift foot and the quick heart, hungry wailing for the days that are no more—till the corrupting apathy that waits for death deepens in his soul, or the nameless horror of death rules him like a tyrant, crying out—" In me there will not even be the memory of fire and joy."

Nor has this dreary old age the powers of manhood in it. For the man having had no youth in his manhood, has had nothing to lift his work over monotony, and when he can do it no more, is weary of it even to sickness, and yet more weary of not having it to do. He misses his labour, yet hates it; strives to do it, but gives up striving. His life is now so empty that, when he is not half mad with the loneliness of doing nothing, he half maddens others with irritability and complaint, with all the misery and misery-making of angry impotence. He has neither fervour of heart, nor capacity for activity—neither youth nor manhood in old age.

And does he serve the Lord? Is he fit to fulfil the perfect work of the last years of life? Not he! He has neither served the Lord through youth nor manhood. He is not likely to do so now with any joy or peace. There are those who cannot begin to search for God if they have neglected Him all their life. It is too late. The ground within is too hard, too beaten down with the trampling of battering days to receive the seed of God; or too choked with the thorns and thistles of selfish worldliness to let the seed grow, even should it creep into the soil. Others do not care. " Death is coming fast. Let me eat and drink," they say, " for to-morrow I die." It is as common a cry in chilly age as in hot-hearted youth. If the old have none of youth's spiritual fervour, they will seek what sensual fervour there may yet be left. If they have no romance within, there is still " savoury venison such as my soul loveth." If they can be active no more to win money, they can console themselves with contemplating it. " At least, I shall die rich," they say, " and to walk among my barns warms my heart." In these lives God does not abide. They cannot serve the Lord; and they die alone, looking out into darkness, insatiably clinging to life like a drowning sailor to the rock against which the waves are breaking him to pieces.

Some, however, do succeed in finding God their Father, though they have not served Him in the past. But with what pain, with what trouble is the work done? For all the hard ground of the old life has to be broken up, and this is terrible work for an old man. Or if he have not the strong nature which needs this rough ploughing, and have a nature either dull or weak, how little joy he has in serving God! How lifeless now are all his efforts! How dimly, as through a window of horn, does he see the celestial city and the face of God! And what regret they both possess. For they have only the dregs of life to offer to their Father; and though He accepts them with infinite love, yet, in proportion as they feel His love, have they the sorrow of loving Him all too late; of having but little fervour to give, little work of which they are now capable. A maimed, imperfect, joyless, regretful old age.

ii. It should be different: it is different for those who have added the serving of the Lord to the ardour of youth, and ennobled with it the business of middle age. God has been dear to them in the past; He is dearer now. Communion with Him has made youth sweeter, brighter, holier; manhood wiser, more loving, more ideal: while tempted, conquering; while troubled, still at peace. And now the hour is come when we may draw still nearer to Him whom we have served all our life long. The noise of life is over, and we can listen, far apart, to the "undisturbèd song of pure concent." The temptations of life are no more. They lie dead, like the Egyptians on the sea-shore, and in our hearts is the song of Miriam—"Sing ye to the Lord, for He hath triumphed gloriously; the horse and his rider hath He thrown into the sea. Not unto us, O Lord, not unto us, but unto Thy name be the praise." The troubles of life are no more trouble. They have been transmuted into inward powers. The cares of life are fled away; they are with God, cast on Him, for He careth for us. All is deep peace; and we say to ourselves as we go to rest each night, and it is both prayer and praise—" He maketh the storm a calm, so that the waves thereof are still. Then are they glad because they are at rest, so He bringeth them to the haven where they would be." Then we know the meaning of

Immanuel—God with us; deep, ineffable, unbroken, eternal communion with God, as of friend with friend, so that we have the dearest affection of manhood with Him; as of Teacher with pupil still, so that we feel young again with Him; as of Father with child, so that, in the winter of age, we walk with Him through the fields of childhood, till, in this communion with Him who is for ever old and for ever young, we know no fixity of feeling as to youth, or middle-age, or old age, but live in that eternity of God which keeps the powers of all the three.

And it is in and through this deep communion that we at last understand that saying of St. Paul's—"Now abideth Faith, Hope, and Charity, these three; but the greatest of these is Charity."

The Hope which was so plentiful in youth is no longer with us in age. It was hope for things belonging to this world, and for our own inner life; and as to the things of this world, we have passed through them; and as to our own inner life, we have attained the things we hoped for when we were young. Hope, therefore, unless we are very anxious to live on—and some have that desire—does not much trouble old age. Or, if we hope, it is not for ourselves, but for others. And, indeed, one of the most beautiful things which can belong to old age, and which is as fair for others to see as it is for the old themselves to feel, is its happy hopefulness for others. It loses all trouble at the defeat of bygone hopes in the joy with which it prophecies the success, and cheers the despondency, of the young. "Let me abide in my own hopes no more," cries the old man "and be troubled with them no more. But in the new hopes of the world, I live. In all the expectations of mankind, in the poetry, romance, dreams, and ideals of youth, I will abide and sympathize."

So also is it with Faith. All that the old man once saw far off, and believed in, is now his own. He has the substance. The eternal world is in him. God needs no proof; for he is in God, and God in him. But, as before it was with hope, so is it now with faith. No longer personal, it passes out of himself and becomes active for others. He believes in men and for men; and his faith for them, living in them, cheers, uplifts, and sends them forward when they faint in the race, or weary in the battle.

But it is not so with Love. Love not only passes from him to the outer world, but abides within him. Indeed, I may express what I have said about hope and faith by saying that they have changed into love; or, better, that they have become new powers of love. Love within, filling the old man's soul, is his very life; felt in silence, when he sits apart as in youthful sunshine; flowing through every memory, kindling in every thought; making tender every book he reads, every soul he meets, every changing of the sky, every music in his ear. For nothing happens hour by hour, into which does not pour, out of the long experiences of feeling, a freshening tide of loving thoughts, of soft and fair associations.

This inner life of love passes from him outwards, and is like a summer atmosphere in which his home and friends are warmed and made more happy; in which sorrows and pains are healed, and mercy poured on wrong, and sins covered, and quarrels laid by, and injuries forgotten. An exquisite gentleness, a mellowed justice, an inexhaustible forgiveness are the old man's heritage; and they are given to all around him, so that they enter into all. This life, so lived, is like an image of God with man; and in truth it is the spirit of the Father rising like light and life from the depths of the old man's heart, and pouring itself forth into the world. One ancient story represents the whole. It was the custom of the disciples of St. John, when he had passed the age of ninety and could scarcely speak to them, to carry the aged apostle every day into the church, and to lay him in their midst. And the old man contented himself with stretching forth his hands towards the crowd, and saying to them, "Little children, love one another." And being asked why he said nothing else, he answered, "That if they truly did so, it were enough."

And in and through all this life is the deepening of personality. None of these things that the old man feels are new, in the sense that they are only now beginning to act, or to be felt. They have acted and been felt from the beginning. Youth has had them; manhood has had them; and now old age has them more fully still. This is their flower. Hence the sense of continuity in life, on which I have already touched, deepens; and, with the feeling that the whole of life is wrought together into one harmonious whole, the conviction of personality is increased. And this personality is felt to be from God, and to abide in God. The old man knows that God has been the living warp upon which the pattern of his life has, from beginning to end, been woven.

And now, what is the deep, the exciting knowledge which

grows out of that conviction of the continuity of personality from youth to age, and out of its divine foundation? It is this—That decay cannot injure or death destroy a life which has cost so much trouble to weave together into continuity. And doubling that conviction, as it were with tenfold proof, is the strange and glorious thing often revealed to us in old age—that neither youth nor manhood are the times in which the graces and gifts which are highest in man reach their full perfection. It is now, now that the man is old, now that decay and death are near, that the best things are in flower—love, mercy, righteousness, joy, peace, humanity—and the more perfect they are, the more they carry with them the conviction of their immortality.

That glorious conviction, now established, makes all these graces and gifts more perfect. And then, old age, that so many vainly pity, goes on its way down hill, upborne by two companions, joy and peace, and feeling in every touch of decay of body, in every warning that death gives, not the approach of dissolution, but a prophecy of everlasting life.

This is old age serving the Lord. It seems to be only contemplation, to be all an inner life. But no! Into this serving of the Lord is carried onwards the activity of manhood. Age has its own business, and it will now be done with activity—business of cheering, of comforting, of impelling, of using experience for help, of being a centre of peace, a living witness to righteousness and the beauty of righteousness, of hoping and believing for others till they believe and hope for themselves. And in all this business the old man is not slothful. For all the habit of his manhood cleaves to him, and to the last he works in this noble and quiet way; and feels again in this bearing into old age of the powers of manhood, the continuity and deepening of personality.

Nor is youth unrepresented.

Its joy remains. The old man's spirit has never ceased to be fervent. Through manhood his youth has lived continuously. Here it is still, in old age. Often, in memory, in dreams, all the romance of early life is present, and his heart beats as fast in age as in the days of old. Still undiminished, even deepened, is the love of beauty. Even in the hour of death the face lights up with joy, thinking of the summer fields and the flying clouds, and the rolling of the sea. And passionate feeling, felt through all beauty, kindled when hearing of some great and noble action, brings tears to the eyes, as warm as those which filled the eyes of youth.

Nor yet do dreams for the future of the world die in old age. They also are here; but they have changed their object. Once they were for the human life of the man himself, and for all he would do; or for the human race, and for all that it would develop in the future. Now, he dreams of all he will be, and of all mankind will be, in the greater, larger world beyond this earth. And these visions are as glorious, as brightly coloured, as the dreams of youth, and far more certain of fulfilment. And as to the ideals to which he aspired when young, he knows he is to find them absolutely fulfilled in the future world. He will touch, and realize, and become at one with perfect self-sacrifice, absolute love, essential truth, eternal knowledge — those divine things which here on earth he knew only in part, and saw, darkly, as through a glass.

So falls on him, while still he is here, the radiance of the other world. In the depths of his soul are all the rapture of youth, all the strength of manhood. Neither youth nor manhood have more excited imaginations, more of all the powers of life, more of all the rushing fire of love, than the old man has now within himself, when, like the sea-king of old, he is laid in the bosom of the ship beneath the mast, with the golden flag flying above his head, and sent forth alone into the sea of eternity to meet God, and with Him to live for ever—not slothful in business; fervent in spirit; serving the Lord.

JUST PUBLISHED.

SUNSHINE AND SHADOW.

Meditations from the Writings
OF THE
REV. STOPFORD A. BROOKE, M.A.

Arranged for Daily Use. With a Photographic Portrait by Elliott & Fry.

Bound in Parchment, price 6s.

DAVID STOTT, 370, OXFORD STREET, W.

www.ingramcontent.com/pod-product-compliance
Lightning Source LLC
Chambersburg PA
CBHW021844230426

43669CB00008B/1081